SECRET STAIRS

A WALKING GUIDE
TO THE
HISTORIC STAIRCASES
OF LOS ANGELES

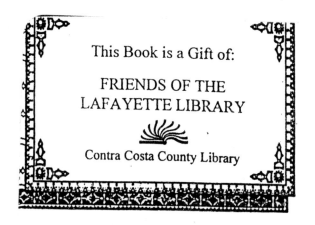

SANTA
MONICA
PRESS

Published by: Santa Monica Press LLC
P.O. Box 1076
Santa Monica, CA 90406-1076
1-800-784-9553
www.santamonicapress.com
books@santamonicapress.com

Printed in the United States

Santa Monica Press books are available at special quantity discounts
when purchased in bulk by corporations, organizations, or groups.
Please call our Special Sales department at 1-800-784-9553.

This book is intended to provide general information. The publisher, author,
distributor, and copyright owner are not engaged in rendering professional
advice or services. The publisher, author, distributor, and copyright owner
are not liable or responsible to any person or group with respect to any loss,
illness, or injury caused or alleged to be caused by the information found in
this book.

ISBN-13 978-1-59580-050-3

Library of Congress Cataloging-in-Publication Data

Fleming, Charles.
  Secret stairs : a walking guide to the historic staircases of Los Angeles / by
Charles Fleming.
    p. cm.
  ISBN 978-1-59580-050-3
  1. Los Angeles (Calif.)—Guidebooks. 2. Staircases—California—Los Angeles—
Guidebooks. 3. Historic sites—California—Los Angeles—Guidebooks.
4. Los Angeles (Calif.)—Buildings, structures, etc.—Guidebooks.
5. Walking—California—Los Angeles—Guidebooks. I. Title.
F869.L83F583 2010
917.94'940454—dc22
                    2009043465

Cover and interior design and production by Future Studio
Cover illustration and maps by Bryan Duddles

Mixed Sources
Product group from well-managed
forests and other controlled sources
www.fsc.org Cert no. SW-COC-002283
© 1996 Forest Stewardship Council
FSC

SECRET STAIRS

A WALKING GUIDE
TO THE
HISTORIC STAIRCASES
OF LOS ANGELES

CHARLES FLEMING

CONTENTS

PART FOUR: HOLLYWOOD AND LOS FELIZ

PART FIVE: SANTA MONICA AND THE WEST

INTRODUCTION

Los Angeles, the city of smog and SigAlerts, is not considered a haven for hikers and walkers. The freeways are full, the surface streets are overcrowded, and the public transit system is feeble. We have almost no pedestrian-friendly, car-free zones and offer our citizens fewer public parks and less public green space per capita than any major city in America.

But Los Angeles, secretly, is a *wonderful* place to walk—if you know where to go.

This book is designed to celebrate urban hiking by exposing the semi-secret network of public staircases that lace the hillsides of certain Los Angeles neighborhoods. The staircases themselves are historical reminders of a time when Los Angeles was *not* a city of cars. City planners and developers installed them as direct routes for pedestrians—housewives and children particularly—to get down the hills to school, the supermarket, and transit lines. The city at that time was well served by trolleys, streetcars, buses, and light-rail systems. The staircases were clustered around steep hillside communities near these transit lines—especially communities that developed in the 1920s like Silver Lake, Echo Park, Mt. Washington, and El Sereno, and the elevated areas of Highland Park, Hollywood, and Santa Monica.

The staircase-to-trolley system was so much a part of the landscape that developers in some areas built houses that had no other access to the outside world. These "walk-streets," several of which appear in this book, were set on hillsides without driveways or garages. Everything going in and out had to employ the public staircase running, usually, across the front of the house.

The trolleys and streetcars are gone, but the staircases remain. Many of them are forgotten paths, neglected and unused. Many of them are also direct routes into stately old Los Angeles neighborhoods that many Angelinos have never even seen.

My first exposure to the staircases was a house on Loma Vista, a walk-street in eastern Silver Lake, where I lived for a short while in 1981. I gradually became aware of other staircases around the area, found them enchanting, and later started walking them in earnest. When I decided to explore and chronicle all the staircases in Silver Lake, and maybe Echo Park, I imagined including about 20 to 25 sets of stairs. I discovered there were more than 60 of them in Silver Lake alone, and at least half that many again in Echo Park. But once I'd started, I didn't know where to stop, so I kept going. Walking in the early mornings, seldom meeting anyone as I hunted staircases, I felt like Henry Hudson searching for the Northwest Passage. Silver Lake walks led into Franklin Hills, which led into Los Feliz, which led into Hollywood. . . .

In the end, I walked, measured, studied, photographed, and mapped more than 275 individual staircases across the Los Angeles area, as far east as Pasadena and as far west as Pacific Palisades.

The original model for this book is a series of circular "pub walk" books I encountered when I first started walking and hiking in England and Ireland. In those slim volumes, the walker is guided on a long country stroll that starts and ends in the parking lot of a public house or restaurant, to which he is encouraged to repair afterward for refreshment and restoration.

Each of the walks in this collection, with one or two exceptions, begins and ends at an easily located café or restaurant that provides food, drink, and other comforts. Each is served by public transport and is measured for distance and difficulty—"one" being a gentle stroll, and "five," a serious hike—and includes the time required and the number of actual staircase steps involved. (The time and distances are approximations.) Many of the shorter walks could be combined to form a longer walk: Silver Lake Terraces—East could join Swan's Way, for example, or Magic Gas could meet Avalon-Baxter and then fold into Fellowship Park. With the exception of a Downtown Los Angeles walk that includes a hotel lobby or two, none of these walks involves any private property. Though some of the city's staircases have periodically been gated or locked by local residents claiming the stairs as their own, they are public byways, on public property, built and maintained by taxpayer dollars, and are meant to be employed and enjoyed by *everyone*.

So, start walking.

PART ONE

PASADENA
AND THE EAST

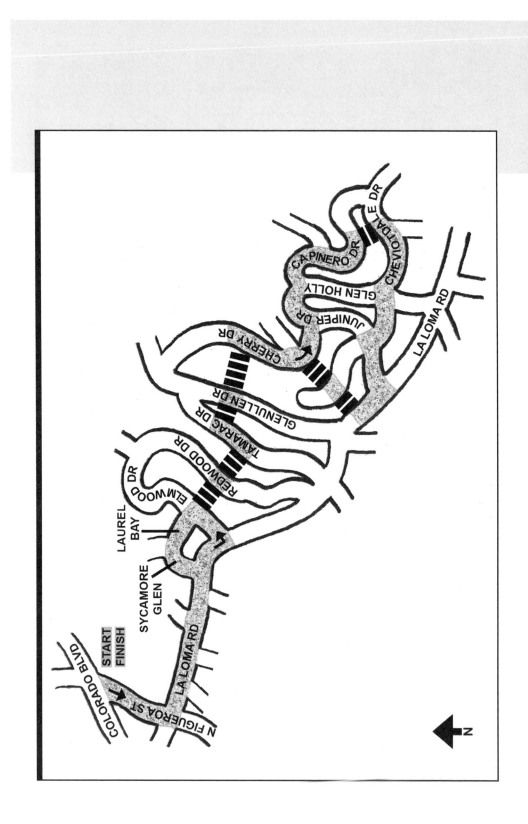

WALK #1

PASADENA—LA LOMA ROAD
DURATION: **1 hour**
DISTANCE: **2.7 miles**
STEPS: **996**
DIFFICULTY: **3**
BUS: **#81, 180, 181, 780**

This is a green, leafy walk through one of Pasadena's western-most neighborhoods, filled with charming stairways and a virtual arboretum of mixed tree varieties. It's one of the city's shadiest walks, too, and an excellent choice for a hot day.

Begin your walk near the intersection of N. Figueroa Street and Colorado Boulevard, just where the community of Eagle Rock ends and Pasadena begins. One block south of Colorado is La Loma Road. Have a Starbucks at the Vons grocery store, or a bite at the McDonald's, and then head east on La Loma.

You'll pass under some tall, high-tension electrical lines on your left and the nearby Lanark Shelby Park on your right. Continue straight on under big sycamore trees as you enter Pasadena and La Loma begins to rise. The sidewalk will end shortly. Take a left, after a bit, onto Elmwood Drive.

Wander along—there's not much to look at—for a block or so. Just before the house at 420, find your first staircase rising to the right. This is a long series of steps and walkways, nicely shaded and sometimes a little overgrown. Climb 98 steps—up the first "loma" that gives this area its name—and land at about 380 Redwood Drive. Cross the street and climb the next set of stairs, another series of risers and walkways, that lifts you 100 steps past a very sleek new home with metal siding and a fine vegetable garden. You land in front of this house, at 365 Tamarac Drive.

Cross the street and jog a few paces to the left. Find the next staircase, going down. This again is a lovely, leafy respite from the heat, crossing under a grove of old oak trees, dropping 86 steps and landing you at 360 Glenullen Drive. Cross the street again, still enjoying the shade, and take the walkway leading to your next flight of stairs. These rise again up a series of staircases and walkways, with some areas a little overgrown and, sometimes, a rather nasty dog behind a fence, up 99 steps. You land at 359 Cherry Drive. Take a right, and enjoy a shady, sloping walk downhill.

I didn't see any cherry trees on Cherry, or any redwood trees on Redwood, but the sheer variety of arboreal options is striking here. There are abundant pine trees, as well as palm, along with all sorts of ficus, laurel, oak, sycamore, juniper, and more. The entire area is bird-ridden and filled with song, and every day I've walked there has been quiet and peaceful.

Just after the house at 431, where Cherry meets Sequoia Drive (no, I didn't see any of those, either), notice a staircase going down on your right, passing a charming English cottage and dropping into some fine, heavy foliage.

But don't go there. Instead, carry on straight ahead, sloping down Cherry and turning left onto Juniper Drive. Follow Juniper through a grove of sleek-trunked eucalyptus, then turn left onto Glen Holly Drive, and right just after onto Capinero Drive—passing a handsome Streamline Moderne on the right and a sleek, tall A-frame on your left. Bear right as Capinero passes Anita Drive—noting the huge oak and private vineyard on the corner lot as you go—and follow Capinero a little farther on.

At the lamppost just after 1428, find the next staircase going down on the right. This is a narrow passage, consisting of several sets of stairs and some sloping concrete walkway, of 44 steps in all. (At the top, note the homemade sand trap and

Astroturf putting green on the right.) It drops you off at 1437 Cheviotdale Drive.

Turn right, and follow Cheviotdale, jogging slightly to the left as it crosses Glen Holly, up to a huge gnarled eucalyptus at the corner of Juniper. Turn left, and follow Juniper downhill to the corner of La Loma.

You're back on the boulevard again. You could shorten this walk and head straight back to Figueroa—but why? Instead, walk just past the mailbox at 1587 and turn right and go up the stairs.

This is the set of stairs you saw earlier from above, at the corner of Cherry and Sequoia. Trot up now, 97 steps over multiple landings, crossing an alley-like extension of Cheviotdale halfway up. At the top of the hill, turn left onto Cherry and climb this tree street a bit. Just past the house at 359, find the top of another staircase you've already climbed. Descend 99 steps to land in the shady nook of Glenullen. Cross the street, and head up the staircase on the other side, climbing 86 steps to Tamarac. Jog a bit to the left and across Tamarac, continuing up the stairs 19 steps to a walkway over the crest, and dropping down 71 steps to land on Redwood. Cross the street, and head on down the last long flight of stairs, falling a final 98 steps to land at 424 Elmwood.

Go straight ahead, onto a downhill block of Laurel Bay Drive. At the first corner, turn left onto Sycamore Glen. After a block more, turn right onto La Loma. After one more block, you'll pass Brixton Road, and find yourself leaving Pasadena and re-entering Los Angeles. A block more, and you're back at Figueroa, and your starting point.

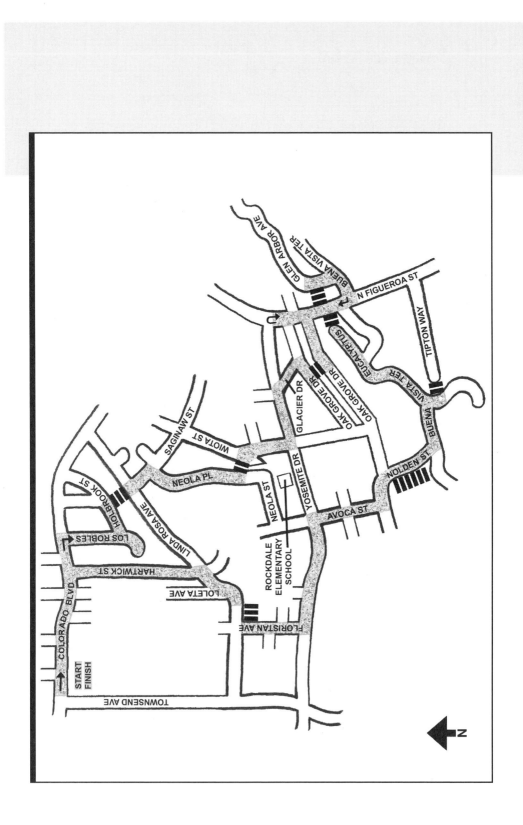

EAGLE ROCK
DURATION: **1 hour, 30 minutes**
DISTANCE: **3.8 miles**
STEPS: **328**
DIFFICULTY: **3**
BUS: **#81, 180, 780**

Here is a relatively gentle walk through a little-known section of a little-known corner of the city, rife with solid local architecture and some of the city's few "sidewalk staircase" streets.

Begin your walk near the corner of Colorado Boulevard and Townsend Avenue, perhaps with a meal at the old-timey Cindy's Restaurant, at 1500 Colorado, or a stop for snacks at Trader Joe's, at 1566 Colorado. When you're done, head east on Colorado, and turn right onto Los Robles Street. Walk to the end of the block, admiring the towering cactus overgrowth on the right, then turn left at Holbrook Street. Gain a little altitude here, and at the T-intersection with Mt. Helena Avenue find your first staircase on the right.

This is a curved staircase with a lovely wrought-iron handrail, built in 1927 by C.W. Ellis. Climb up 31 stairs to a walkway, take another eight stairs and another sloping walkway over the crest, and then drop down 21 stairs to land at the corner of Linda Rosa Avenue and Saginaw Street. Walk straight across the intersection and down Saginaw for one block, then turn right onto Neola Place.

You won't find much to amuse you on this block, as Neola narrows and begins to descend. Near the bottom, the houses get older and more interesting, and Rockdale Elementary School appears down below. Just after the house at 1840, find the next staircase, to your left. Drop down 47 stairs, with rails and an overhead light, to the back of the schoolyard, where you'll land on Neola Place. Walk a block straight ahead, to the corner of Wiota Street, then turn right again and walk a single block to Yosemite Drive.

Cross at the light and turn left onto Yosemite, and walk one long block and turn right onto Glacier Drive. At the next corner, look to the right and find your next staircase—a short stretch of 20 steps, with a handrail, connecting the upper and lower sections of Oak Grove Drive. Enjoy the overhang of the trees that give the road its name, and turn left. After one block, at Figueroa Street, turn left again and walk back to Yosemite. Use the traffic light to cross to the opposite side of Figueroa, and turn right. Head back up the hill a half block and find the next staircase on your left.

This is a monumental set of stairs, decorated with a mu-ral of Tai Chi students, employing 64 steps and a concrete slope to land on Glen Arbor Avenue. Turn right and head downhill, then turn right again onto Buena Vista Terrace. After a block, on Figueroa once more, cross at the crosswalk and turn right, head-ing back downhill on Figueroa toward Yosemite. After about a block, just opposite the Tai Chi steps you just climbed, find your next staircase at the turning for Eucalyptus Lane.

This is a short stretch of 39 stairs, depositing you at the barricaded end of an unusually rustic Los Angeles lane. The feel-ing here is more Topanga Canyon than Eagle Rock. The houses are old and somewhat ramshackle, and the trees and vines are old and overgrown. Walk straight ahead to the end of Eucalyp-tus. Where it bumps up against Buena Vista Terrace, again, bear right—keeping the white wooden fence on your left. Buena Vista hugs the hillside, remaining shady and pleasantly funky. There are big eastern views as you walk along, to the hills of El Sereno and beyond.

At the first corner, turn left onto Tipton Terrace. Walk 100 feet and observe the next staircase on your left—a broken-down wooden staircase with a ramp, connecting Tipton Terrace to Tipton Way. Drop down the 15 ancient steps.

For a shortened version of this walk, you could follow Tipton to the bottom of the hill, turn left onto Figueroa, follow Figueroa back to Colorado, and turn left. That will lead you to the starting point.

Better, though, to climb back up those 15 steps, turn right onto Tipton Terrace, turn left onto Buena Vista Terrace, and continue. Climb up and over the slight rise, and down the other side, and then turn right at the first corner, onto Nolden Street.

This is a steep residential street, so steep that the city engineers supplied a "sidewalk staircase" on the left—a series of 79 steps built into the sidewalk, as Nolden descends to Oak Grove Dr. At the bottom of the hill, after admiring the elevated tree house on the left, turn left onto Oak Grove. Enjoy the flat, shady walk along a street of fine, small Craftsman cottages. Turn right on Avoca Street, walk three blocks, and turn left onto Yosemite. Cross when it's safe, then turn right onto Floristan Avenue. Two blocks up, turn right onto Linda Rosa, and begin the final flight of stairs—another "sidewalk staircase" that carries you up a series of 36 steps, spread over the width of five or six house lots, depositing you at the top of the hill. Almost. Turn left, as Linda Rosa rises turns briefly into Loleta, then bear right as Linda Rosa resumes. At the first turning to the left, drop onto Hartwick Street, and enjoy a sneaky view of downtown Glendale, on the left. Then begin the descent, past a number of nicely preserved older homes, down to Colorado Blvd. Ahead and above is a stretch of the I-210 freeway. Ahead and below, as you meet Colorado, is your starting point.

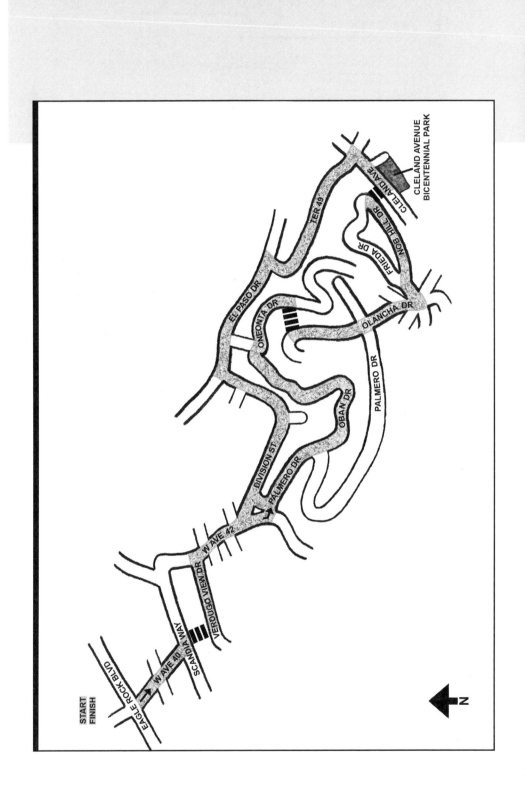

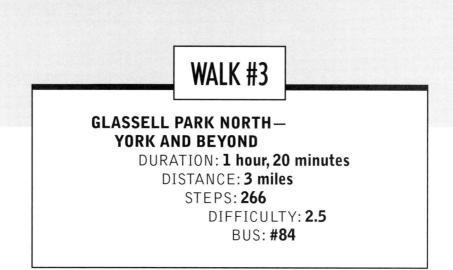

WALK #3

GLASSELL PARK NORTH—
YORK AND BEYOND
DURATION: **1 hour, 20 minutes**
DISTANCE: **3 miles**
STEPS: **266**
DIFFICULTY: **2.5**
BUS: **#84**

This is a long, lopsided loop through one of the city's least-known neighborhoods, featuring ancient wooden staircases and, towering views of the San Gabriel Mountains, Occidental College, and the hidden back side of Forest Lawn Memorial Park.

Begin your walk along the southern end of Eagle Rock Boulevard, near the intersection of Avenue 40, perhaps with a breakfast or lunch at the retro eatery Auntie Em's Kitchen, up the street past York at 4616 Eagle Rock. Finish digesting, then head east on Avenue 40.

Two short blocks in, where Avenue 40 dead-ends into Scandia Way, you'll find your first staircase. This is a rare wooden staircase, not in very good repair, but an interesting throwback to the days when all of the city's public walks were built from timber. (There are a few still extant—like the Adelaide steps in Santa Monica Canyon, the Oak Glen Place steps in Echo Park, and the mighty Eldred steps in Highland Park.) This one runs a quick 25 steps up, lined with wobbly wooden handrails, then follows a steep paved walkway through a grove of fruit trees to a final 10 steps and another set of wobbly rails, to drop you at 4001 Verdugo View Drive. Take a left, and walk along Verdugo to the corner of Avenue 42, and take a right.

This is the dull part of the walk. Stroll along Avenue 42, and go straight ahead through the slightly complicated inter-section, until you are on Palmero Drive. Continue on Palmero until it meets Oban Drive, and then bear left. Follow Oban. The houses gradually become a little more interesting, the greenery and shade get deeper, and the hillsides get steeper. Press on, enjoying the relative quiet, until Oban meets Oneonta Drive. Bear right, following Oneonta around and up, to just past the large orange house at 1109. Here is your second set of stairs.

This is a giant staircase of relatively recent construc-tion, a zigzag design with a double-L base and solid handrails all the way to the top—which is 132 steps straight up. The rigorous climb is broken up by several landings, affording great views of Occidental College and the San Gabriel Mountains. It's also a nicely shaded walk, thanks to some young oak trees planted here, and a pair of grand date palms at the crest.

You've landed at 1100 Olancha Drive. Off to the right, down the hill, across the Glendale Freeway, you will see a vast expanse of greenery. This is the back side of Forest Lawn Me-morial Park. Don't go there, though. Instead, turn left and walk along Olancha, enjoying some good shady overhang and in-creasingly interesting houses. You'll also begin to see "No on 710" signs, evidence of the fierce local resistance to the long-planned, long-stalled proposal to extend the Long Beach Free-way from its current terminus, near the I-10 freeway, by Cal State Los Angeles, to the I-210 freeway in Pasadena.

Ahead is a complex, six-way intersection. Take a hard left onto N. Nob Hill Drive, and then bear right at the fork, heading downhill. Here again are big mountain views as the street heads north, crests and begins to drop. At the bottom of the hill, just past the house 4832, find the next staircase on your right.

Like its Scandia Way cousin, this one is a wooden struc-ture, composed of 17 initial steps, a long sloping walkway with good shade, and 47 concluding steps. You land at 4841 Cleland Avenue, across the street from Cleland Avenue Bicentennial Park. Turn left, go to the corner at Terrace 49, and turn left again.

Here are some older homes, including a few with curious Japanese lettering and one with a handsome *torii* gate and pensive Buddha statue. Near the end of the block, at 971, there is an unexpected group of redwood trees.

Terrace 49 ends at El Paso Drive. Turn left, and follow El Paso down a bit, turning left again onto Division Street. Follow Division along until it brings you back to the intersection with Avenue 42. Turn right, go the three blocks to Verdugo View, and turn left. Just past the house at 4001, you'll find your original staircase heading down on the right. Go straight at the bottom of the stairs, back to Eagle Rock Blvd. and your starting point.

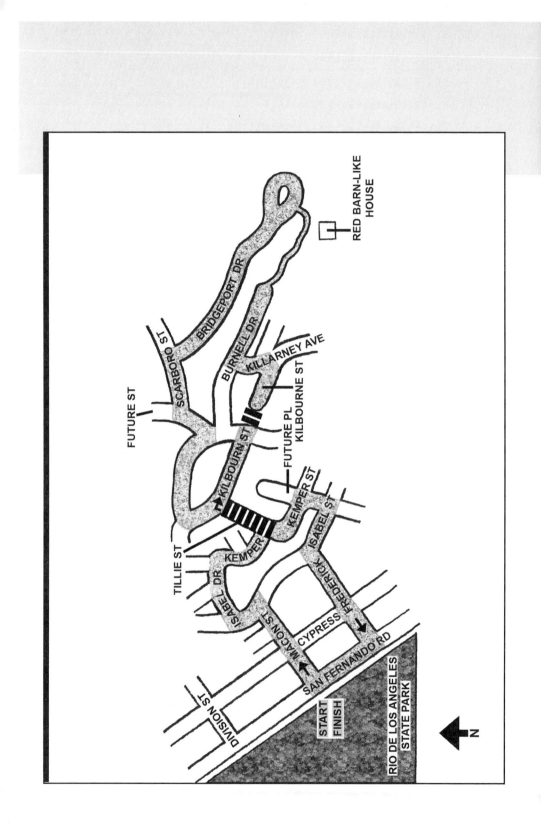

GLASSELL PARK SOUTH—TAYLOR YARD
DURATION: **1 hour, 15 minutes**
DISTANCE: **3.2 miles**
STEPS: **401**
DIFFICULTY: **3**
BUS: **#90, 91, 94**

Here's a nifty trip through the Mt. Washington-adjacent hills, with a starting point by the Los Angeles River and a stroll through an unexpected piece of Santa Monica Conservancy parkland.

Begin your walk at Rio de Los Angeles State Park—in what used to be the railroad switching station known as Taylor Yard—on N. San Fernando Road near Division Street. Leave the park, cross San Fernando and walk up Macon Street. Cross Cypress Avenue—carefully, as there is no crosswalk here—and continue up Macon to Isabel Street. Take a left, then a right almost immediately onto Isabel Drive. Walk straight ahead until Isabel bumps into Kemper Circle, and bear right.

Behind you, there are low-altitude views of Taylor Yard and of Elysian Park. Ahead, there are remnants of an old private staircase or two. Follow Kemper up and around, enjoying the increasingly good views, until just before 3014. Take the Tillie Street stairs to your left, and start climbing.

This is one of the city's few true walk-streets—the houses here can only be accessed by the stairways—rising a total of 135 steps, courtesy of builders MacDonald and Kahn, and inspector W.E. Moyle, from 1928. The staircase is outfitted with sturdy handrails, is well maintained, and drops you off at 1750 Kilbourn Street. Take a right, and walk downhill the length of a city block.

At the bottom, find your next staircase, directly across the intersection with Future Street. This one climbs 133 steps, and again is equipped with good rails and great views—from the third landing up you can see as far west as the Griffith Observatory—and culminates at the cul-de-sac end of West Kilbourn. Walk a block straight ahead, and turn left onto Killarney Avenue.

You're at the back side of Mt. Washington now. Crest the hill in front of you, and pass Randall Court, and turn right at the next corner onto Burnell Drive. Walk off the pavement and onto the dirt road and you are in Elyria Canyon, parkland controlled by the Santa Monica Conservancy.

This is an unexpected pleasure in the middle of the city, and it's full of trails and walkways and a fantastic variety of indigenous trees. (There are also indigenous dangers: Signs further into the park warn you to watch out for rattlesnakes and poison oak.) For now, walk straight ahead along the dirt road, pass a metal swing gate, and continue on the path beyond. Where it comes to a T-intersection, take the trail heading down and left, toward a wide dirt road heading to the left and a red barn-like house down to the right. Go toward the house, and circle around behind it. Here, you will find a freestone drinking fountain, a park bench, and some welcome shade. There are also trailheads here, leading up and around the edges of the canyon.

When you have fed and watered the horses, return to the path by the red house, taking the wider dirt road heading to the right. Up ahead you will see a set of green gates. Pass through these and leave the park, back onto paved road, via Bridgeport Drive. Down the hill, turn left onto Scarboro Street. Climb up a bit, turn left again onto another stretch of Future St., and after another climb turn right at the first corner. There's no sign for it, but this is the extension of Burnell Dr. Make your last climb up Burnell, admiring the fine freestone stairway on the left at 1842.

At the next corner, turn left onto Kilbourn. Just past 1804, find the Tillie St. stairway going down to the right. At the bottom, turn left onto Kemper. Watch for oncoming cars—this road turns into a narrow alley, and has no sidewalk. At the bottom of the bend, turn right onto yet another stretch of Future St. Turn right onto Isabel. Turn left onto Frederick Street, past a collection of sad stucco bungalows, and cross Cypress carefully once more. At San Fernando, turn right, and find your way back to Macon and the gate to Taylor Yard.

If you have time, enjoy the facilities. The park offers tennis and basketball courts, baseball and soccer fields, a play area, a small water park, drinking fountains, a cold soda machine, restrooms and a network of trails leading down to the old train yard. You'll hear the lonesome whistle of a freight train as you recover from the walk.

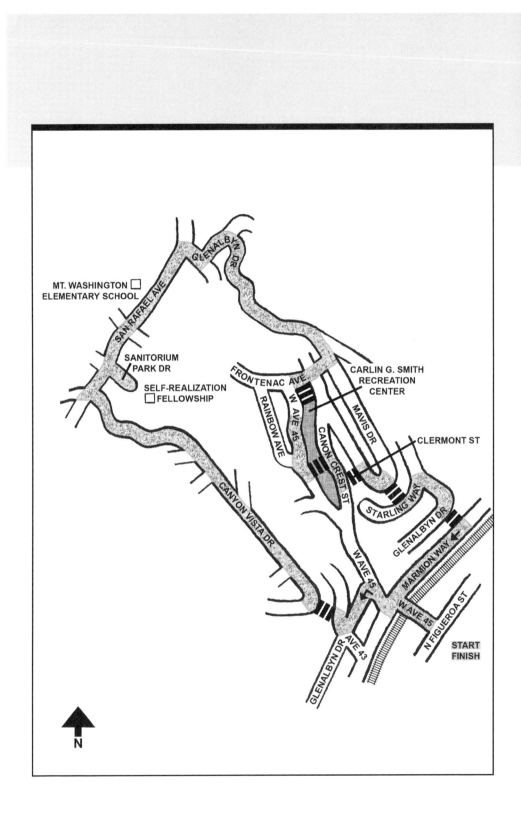

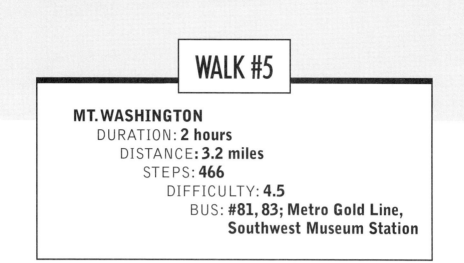

WALK #5

MT. WASHINGTON
DURATION: **2 hours**
DISTANCE: **3.2 miles**
STEPS: **466**
DIFFICULTY: **4.5**
BUS: **#81, 83; Metro Gold Line,
Southwest Museum Station**

*This is a green, leafy walk through one of Pasadena's western-
most neighborhoods, filled with charming stairways and a
virtual arboretum of mixed tree varieties. It's one of the city's
shadiest walks, too, and an excellent choice for a hot day.*

Begin the walk near the intersection of N. Figueroa Street and
Avenue 45, perhaps with a cool drink from Taco Fiesta or a hot
coffee from Yum Yum Donut. Walk up Avenue 45, cross the Gold
Line tracks and Marmion Way, and then jog left a bit and go up
and left onto Glenalbyn Drive. Walk to Avenue 43. Down and to
the left, you will notice two cream-colored, arch-roofed Spanish Mission Revival-style buildings. These are all that remains
of an old funicular railway that, from 1884 until about 1920, carried passengers from Figueroa St. to the top of Mt. Washington,
and the Mt. Washington Hotel. These buildings housed some of
the machinery for the railway.

Turn away from that to the right, and walk up one short,
steep block of Avenue 43, and find the first staircase, on your
left.

This is a zigzag set of 102 steps over seven landings, with

a handrail but no lights, bordered by a nice cactus garden. At the top, you land on Canyon Vista Drive. From here, it's a steep climb straight up. (You will see why the Mt. Washington Hotel folks built a railway.) Climb and climb, past the turnings for Glenwood Avenue, Frontenac Avenue, and Camino Real. Where the road splits, keep to the right-hand, uphill side. (Don't head downhill here into the canyon.) Behind you are excellent views of El Sereno. Down to your left, into the eucalyptus-lined canyon, are views of Downtown and East Los Angeles. The huge building you see rising above the others is Los Angeles County Hospital, which at the time of its construction in 1933 was said to be the largest medical facility west of the Mississippi.

At the stop sign, turn right onto San Rafael Avenue. A hundred feet in, turn right again onto Sanitorium Park Drive and through the gates of the Self-Realization Fellowship.

This is the old Mt. Washington Hotel, sold to the SRF and opened as a meditation and teaching center in 1925. Today the gentle followers of Paramahansa Yogananda welcome you to their exquisite gardens, and invite you to visit the shrine to their founder. The gardens are open Tuesday to Friday, 9:00 AM to 4:30 PM, Saturday from 11:00 AM to 4:30 PM, and Sunday from 1:00 PM to 4:30 PM. (The grounds are also open Monday, but some areas may be closed for maintenance.)

Restored, leave the gardens, return to San Rafael Ave., and go right and downhill. Enjoy good northern views as you pass the turn for Rome Drive. Enjoy the shade of the overhanging oak trees, and the fine old Craftsman at 3923.

(If you are a staircase fanatic, walk past Mt. Washington Elementary School and turn left onto Danforth Drive. Walk to the end of the road. There at the cul-de-sac is a beautifully crafted set of stairs and walkways designed to deliver school children to and from the newish development on Marchena Street below. The staircase has no particular application for the purpose of this walk, but it's an engineering wonder. If you wished to connect this walk to Walk #4, these stairs would be the way to do it.)

If you're just an average staircase fanatic, stay on San Rafael on past Mt. Washington Elementary School, and then turn right onto Glenalbyn Drive. Watch the turns that come next: Bear left at the Lark Court intersection, then bear right at Quail Drive, still following Glenalbyn down and around, as the street gets steeper and the views improve.

Where the road splits again, leave Glenalbyn and bear right, onto Mavis Drive. At the first corner, turn right onto Frontenac Avenue. Walk one block, across Avenue 46, and then watch for the stairs on your left into the Carlin G. Smith Recreation Center—through a little swing gate just before you hit Avenue 45. (If the gate is locked, continue along Frontenac to Avenue 45, turn left, and walk down to meet the trail just after the basketball court.) Walk down 16 steps, through another gate straight ahead, down another six steps and a ramp, then catch the zigzag set of 31 stairs falling down into the playground. Walk toward the basketball court, where you'll find a most welcome drinking fountain, and exit off to the left side. Turn right at once, and cross the canyon, walking along the fence line. Join Avenue 45, turn left, and head downhill.

Walk carefully here. The street is steep and there is no sidewalk. Keep the gully on your left. Then, where Rainbow Avenue comes in on the right, cross into the gully, under the trees, and find the next staircase.

This is a short set of 22 asphalt steps, with a handrail. Turn right onto Canon Crest Avenue, then almost immediately turn left onto the Clermont Street staircase—another of the city's true walk-streets. Truck up the 10 landings and the 154 steps here, without lights or handrails, all the way to the top—pausing part of the way for great views of East Los Angeles.

You emerge at 438 West Avenue 46. Turn right and head downhill, as the road turns into Mavis Dr. and winds down and around to the left. Here, pay close attention. Just after the house and fence at 330, find your next staircase going down to the right. This is a railroad-tie staircase in relatively poor repair, running through a lovely low-hanging grove that looks like private property—but isn't. Drop down 37 wooden steps, 11 earthen steps, and finish with 28 concrete steps to land at 4581 Starling Way. Turn left, head downhill, and then hang a hairpin turn right back onto Glenalbyn Dr.

Slope down, gradually losing all the altitude you've earned, enjoying the shade and some of the fine old houses, like the huge Craftsman at 4591. Just after that, watch for the final staircase on the left side. This is a newish set of 59 steps, with handrails and very attractive lamps, dropping you down from Glenalbyn to Marmion Way.

You land at 4601 Marmion Way, just across from the Gold Line's Southwest Museum Station. For a side visit, go left and see the museum. (But only if it's the one Saturday per month that the museum is open.) Otherwise, turn right and head downhill, noticing as you pass the fine-looking freestone garages at 4579, and the old "Garden House" apartment building just beyond. Walk down to Avenue 45, and return to your starting point.

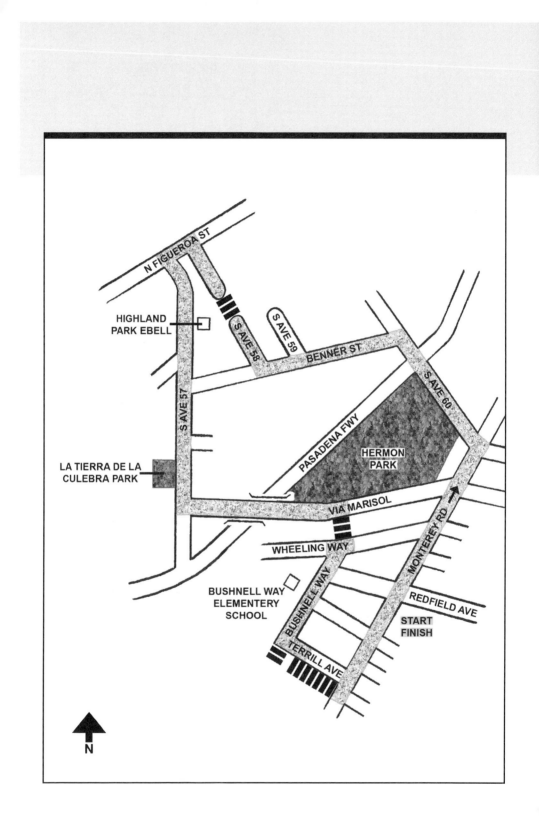

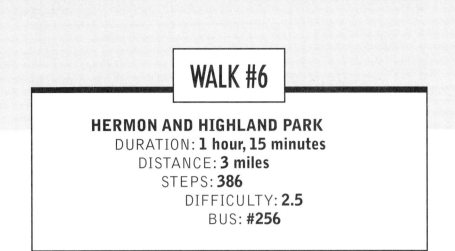

WALK #6

HERMON AND HIGHLAND PARK
DURATION: **1 hour, 15 minutes**
DISTANCE: **3 miles**
STEPS: **386**
DIFFICULTY: **2.5**
BUS: **#256**

This is a quirky walk through a quirky part of town—most Angelinos don't even know there is a Hermon—featuring some very secluded staircases and some ancient Los Angeles history.

Begin your walk in Hermon, near the intersection of Via Marisol and Monterey Road, perhaps with a fresh beverage from Cycleway Coffee, at 5526 Monterey. The café features wall-sized photographs of the elevated wooden cycle freeway a local entrepreneur built in the nearby arroyo, running from Pasadena's Green Hotel into Downtown Los Angeles. The photographs are all that remains of the historic cycleway, which opened in 1890 and closed shortly after.

Start walking north on Monterey toward Via Marisol, admiring the old frame houses along the way. Cross Via Marisol, and enter historic Hermon, a townlet dating from 1903, when a group of Methodists built a church school here. (The school became Los Angeles Pacific College, then became Pacific Christian Preparatory School, and then closed.) Continue to the next intersection, and turn left onto S. Avenue 60. Cross the Pasadena Freeway, also known as the Historic Arroyo Seco Parkway.

Then turn left onto Benner Street. Walk along, as the noise of the freeway diminishes, taking note of the two or three really old clapboard homes still standing. Cross Avenue 59, and then turn right on S. Avenue 58.

Dead ahead, past a row of depressing houses and a yard full of angry dogs, find your first staircase. This is an elegantly designed staircase of recent construction, marching up 80 steps over multiple landings, with rails and lights and a shady over-hang of eucalyptus. You land at the other side of S. Avenue 58. Walk straight ahead a half block, again appreciating the nicely preserved wood frame homes, and turn left onto N. Figueroa Street.

This block runs through the middle of Highland Park and has a distinctly old-time feel: There's a typewriter repair shop, a decades-old camera shop and, down the road a bit, the historic Highland Theater. Walk a block, and turn left again onto S. Avenue 57.

On the left you'll pass the Highland Park Ebell, a 1912 building erected by an elite women's club organized in 1903. Freestone walls line older homes on the block, and freestone chimneys accompany a few. Further along, at the corner of Me-dia Drive, you'll find one of the neighborhood's oldest homes, a turn-of-the-century frame house with substantial groves of eucalyptus, oak, and avocado trees. Further still, on your right, is a marvelous urban oasis known as La Tierra de la Culebra Park, an open-to-the-public garden operated by the non-profit Arts Community Land Activism organization. The park, built on the ruins of several old homes, features rock walls, terraced rock gardens, tile-lined rock pools and a surfeit of oaky shade. There's a coffeehouse, too—Ghetto Grounds—that helps raise revenue for the park.

Past La Culebra, continue along Avenue 57 to the in-tersection with Via Marisol. Bear left, and take the bridge back over the Arroyo Seco Parkway—noting, below, the more modern concrete cycleway the city has built at the flat bottom of the dry riverbed. On the other side of the freeway, to the left, is Hermon Park, which offers tennis courts, play areas, dog runs, and public restrooms. Midway up the park, take the pedestrian crosswalk to the southern side of Via Marisol. A few feet past the crosswalk find your next staircase.

This is a fine wide staircase, lighted, without handrail, but equipped on the left-hand side with an admirable collection of roosters and chickens. Enjoy their squawking and crowing as you climb up 62 stairs, over multiple landings, to arrive on Wheeling Way. Take this to the right, where the roadway bears left and turns into Bushnell Way.

Bushnell rises to a slight slope, passing the corners of Redfield Avenue and Kendall Avenue, passing the large beige-colored Bushnell Way Elementary School, then swings left and turns into Terrill Avenue. Here, at the turning, find your next staircase.

Such peace and tranquility! Such understated elegance! And, for what? This lovely staircase, which rises up 104 steps, turns left, and becomes a sloping walkway, goes nowhere. It parallels Terrill Ave., and is actually a city block of Pullman Street, and might once have served a community of homes higher up the slope, but there are no homes to serve anymore, and the staircase goes . . . nowhere. The steps rise another 22 steps, and the walkway continues. Just here, at a break in the dense overhang of coast live oak trees, there are suddenly good views of the arroyo, Pasadena, and the San Gabriel Mountains. The walkway continues, and then meets the stairs going down 140 steps, with lights and handrails, over multiple landings to drop you at the other end of Terrill.

You are actually standing, though, at the base of Walnut Hill. The road below you is the Monterey Rd. pass, which cut through Walnut Hill in 1930 and connected Hermon to the communities of Happy Valley and El Sereno, to the south.

Turn left, and walk back down onto Monterey Rd. A few blocks along, you'll find Redfield, Cycleway Coffee, and your starting point.

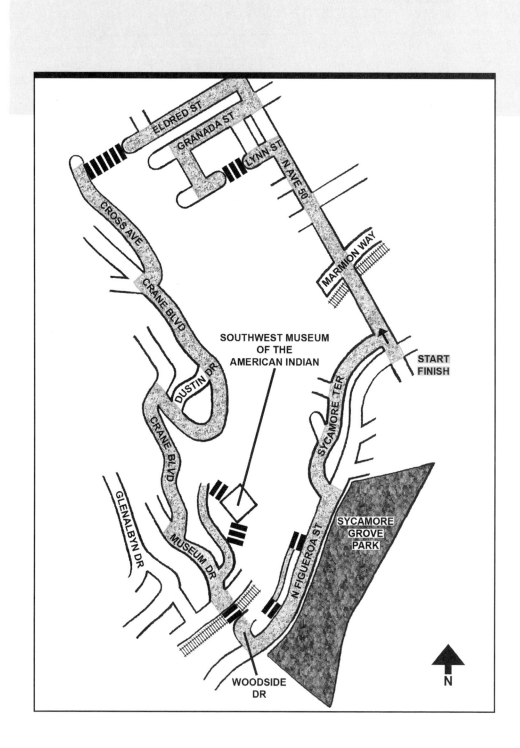

HIGHLAND PARK—SOUTHWEST MUSEUM
DURATION: **1 hour, 30 minutes**
DISTANCE: **3.2 miles**
STEPS: **568**
DIFFICULTY: **5**
BUS: **#81, 83**

Like its Mt. Washington neighbor in Walk #5, this is more a hike than a walk—up a very steep staircase, down some very steep hills, with as much elevation change as any staircase walk in Los Angeles. But the payoff: huge views, a sneaky approach to the Southwest Museum of the American Indian, and a visit to some amazing hillside streets.

Begin this walk near the intersection of N. Figueroa Street and N. Avenue 50, in the heart of Highland Park, perhaps with a coffee from McDonald's or a meal from Chico's Mexican Restaurant, both on that corner. Begin walking west on Avenue 50. Cross the Gold Line subway track at Marmion Way. Walk on, past Monte Vista Street and Malta Street. Then turn left on Lynn Street, and walk to the end of the block. Here, you'll find your first staircase—dropping down 60 paces over three landings, with handrails and lights, and depositing you at the continuation of Lynn. Walk a block, and turn right onto N. Avenue 49.

This is an odd little canyon of tidy, single-family homes, many dating from the 1920s. Walk a block of Avenue 49, and turn right again onto Granada Street. Walk up a slight rise, past another collection of modest older homes, and turn left onto Avenue 50. After one block, turn left and head down Eldred Street.

Enjoy the slight downhill; it won't last. Eldred flattens out and begins heading uphill, then gets quite steep. At the corner of Avenue 48, it gets very steep indeed. Walk slowly, past the lovely handwritten signs that say, "Mt. Washington 0.6 miles" and "Watch for Children, Big Horn Sheep, Loose Dogs & Motorcycles." After a block's worth of very steep walking, under the shade of some Chinese pepper and oak trees, find your next staircase.

This is the granddaddy of wooden staircases, an old construction made new again after a 2009 restoration. It is equipped with sturdy handrails, and rises—gently at first, and then not so gently—a towering 196 steps. The climb is somewhat shaded by trees and serenaded by roosters, and offers increasingly impressive views of Highland Park, Pasadena, Altadena, Mt. Wilson, Mt. Baldy, and beyond.

At the top of the stairs, you land at 700 Cross Avenue. Down to the right, at the wooden barricades, the views are even better. When you've enjoyed those, and caught your breath, head back past the staircase, and on up the hill.

For the next mile or so you will be treated to a very pleasant walk. Cross Avenue hugs the hillside, offering grand views of the city below and the mountains beyond, as it winds along. Where it meets Crane Boulevard, turn left, and continue along as the road begins to descend slightly. The way is shadier here, and the trees seem full of bird life. (Overhead, hawks twirl.) The houses are a charming mix of old shingle and clapboard, side-by-side with newer Spanish or stucco.

At the next turning, where Crane meets Dustin Drive, bear left and stay on Crane. As the road drops and bends right, the views become really striking. Suddenly below is the back side of the Southwest Museum, and beyond that, the Arroyo Seco, and beyond *that*, the Audubon Society's Center at Ernest Debs Regional Park—a grand place for a full bird-watching expedition. As you continue around the bend, you get views of City Hall and the Downtown skyline.

Crane passes the other side of Dustin, and begins a sharper descent. At the next turning, for Rustic Drive, make a sharp hairpin left, and stay on Crane as it continues downhill.

The road here begins to take on a Laurel Canyon or Topanga Canyon feel. Note the garage shrine at 368, the Spanish bell tower at 334, and the stately older clapboard at 312, built in 1924. Note also, high above on the right, the stretch of Glenalbyn Drive you might have already experienced on Walk #5.

Crane elbows into Museum Drive at the bottom of the hill. Turn left onto Museum, and after a short stretch, find a surprise. On the left, marked with the number 234, is a strange secret entrance to the Southwest Museum of the American Indian.

Behind these imposing stone gates is a 200-foot-long tunnel, constructed in 1920, leading to an elevator that rises to the interior of the museum high above. Alas, it is seldom open—unless you are part of a private group tour and have made reservations. Walk up the nine steps to its door, then turn right and walk along the sidewalk to the museum driveway. Turn left into the drive, and follow the sign for "Hopi Trail" on the right. This is your next staircase, a flagstone walkway with a handrail that will carry you 100 steps up to a flat area with benches for resting, and another 16 railroad-tie steps to the base of the museum, another 19 to the museum's main plaza, and a final 17 to the museum's front door. *Whew.*

But don't stop. The museum is only open one Saturday a month. If you're not there that Saturday, walk back down the steps past the cannon, back down the next flight of stairs, and then turn up to the right, keeping the museum building on your right-hand side, heading uphill on the sidewalk. This meets an asphalt driveway. Go up the driveway a bit, and then turn right into a little plaza. Here, you will find big comfortable chairs and benches, and the Braun Research Library. Just past that, on the left, you'll also find a set of 23 stairs. Rise up, cross the driveway, and walk over to the right. There's a charming, small amphitheater there, with seats and great views of the San Gabriel Mountains.

When you decide to leave the amphitheater, cross the parking lot, heading downhill and to the right. Follow the driveway exit to the left, and head down the slope to leave the museum. Down below on the right, you can see the top of the tunnel you passed on Museum Dr. Shortly, you'll come to the "Hopi Trail" on the left. Just after that, turn left onto the sidewalk and go to the corner. Cross Marmion Way, and find the staircase down into the Gold Line's Southwest Museum Station.

This is a short set of 11 steps delivering you right to the tracks. Open the swing gate, cross the tracks—carefully, mindful of the signals announcing the approaching trains since the gates do not lock when a train is coming—and take the next set of stairs. This is a longer set of 27 steps, and a long sloping ramp, that will drop you onto Woodside Drive. Walk straight ahead, almost to the corner of N. Figueroa, and turn left—up a set of 16 wide stone stairs to the sidewalk above.

This is a lovely elevated walkway watching over N. Figueroa and Sycamore Grove Park. On your left will be the Southwest Museum's Casa de Adobe, a 1918 construction, designed to look like a pre-1850 Los Angeles home. (It is currently closed to the public.) As you walk along, beneath fine examples of coast live oak, you'll pass a series of nice, old stucco bungalow homes and several excellent examples of Craftsman architecture.

In time, you'll come to a very elegant T-shaped staircase. Walk down 12 steps, and back up 28, pausing to admire the sanctuary of the Virgin Mary in the middle. On the other side, you'll get good views of Sycamore Grove Park, including a small amphitheater with outdoor seating.

The sidewalk will end in a sweeping staircase to Figueroa. Take the 46 steps down, and turn left onto the busy boulevard. At the first turning, for Sycamore Terrace, pause to admire the deeply charming Hiner House and Sousa Nook. This was the 1922 home—a stone and timber "cottage," designed by architect Carl Boller—of Dr. Edward M. Hiner, a popular band leader so enamored of marching band music that he dedicated his rehearsal space in honor of his friend, John Philip Sousa. The peculiar front gate, with its billiard-ball ornamentation, is not part of the Boller design, but the amphitheater you saw earlier is called the Hiner-Sousa Bandshell.

Turn left onto Sycamore Terrace. Walk uphill as the alley-like lane winds through the trees. Bear right onto the sidewalk in front of the vintage Craftsman house at 4925. Ahead you will find some fine freestone walls and walkways accompanying houses in varying states of decay, but culminating in three excellent examples of shingle-sided Craftsman beauty. As the block ends, cross Figueroa and return to your starting point.

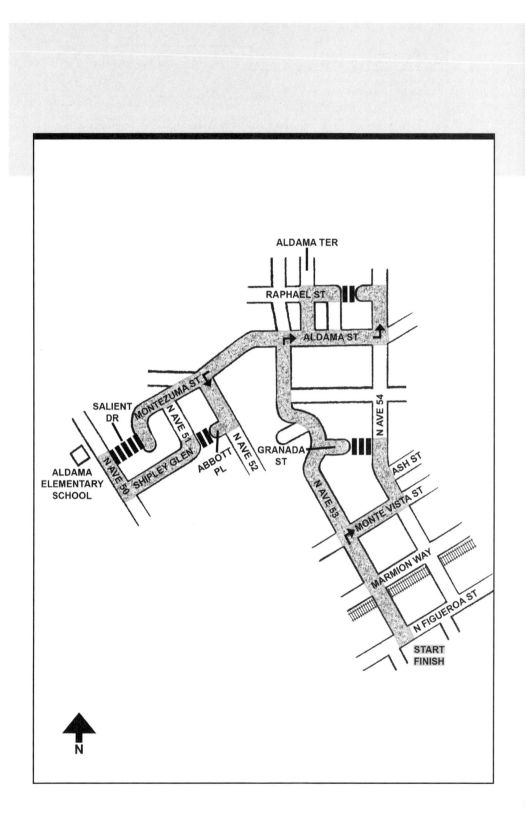

ALDAMA TER

RAPHAEL ST

ALDAMA ST

SALIENT DR

MONTEZUMA ST

N AVE 51

N AVE 54

N AVE 50

SHIPLEY GLEN

ABBOTT PL

N AVE 52

GRANADA ST

ALDAMA ELEMENTARY SCHOOL

N AVE 53

ASH ST

MONTE VISTA ST

MARMION WAY

N FIGUEROA ST

START FINISH

N

HIGHLAND PARK—HIGHLANDS
DURATION: **1 hour, 30 minutes**
DISTANCE: **3.2 miles**
STEPS: **342**
DIFFICULTY: **3**
BUS: **#81, 83, 256**

Here is a sprightly walk through some gorgeous Highland Park neighborhoods, featuring dramatic Craftsman homes, magnificent San Gabriel Views and exposure to some heavy East-meets-West mysticism.

Begin your walk near the intersection of N. Figueroa St. and Avenue 53, perhaps with a carne asada taco from Metro Balderas, at 5305 N. Figueroa, or with a bit of spiritual enlightenment: Along this stretch of the Historic Route 66 are a fine-looking old brick Faith United Presbyterian Church, a huge Mystic Dharma Buddhist Temple, and the world headquarters of the Builders of the Adytum. This spiritualist group, founded in Los Angeles in 1930, bases its occult readings on the Qabalah. "Adytum" is a Greek word meaning "inner shrine," the development of which BOTA followers believe is the purpose of human life.

Thus fortified, within and without, begin by heading north on Avenue 53, along the side of the big Presbyterian church, heading for the hills. Cross the Gold Line tracks at Marmion Way, admiring the little period bungalows as you go—including the one at 215, a Charles Shattuck design from 1906—and turn right onto Monte Vista Street. Here, the Craftsman homes are larger and more elaborate. Turn left, at the next block, onto N. Avenue 54. Just ahead, past the turning for Ash Street, find a break in the long freestone wall on your left, looking for the sign indicating the 5300 block of Granada Street, and find your first staircase.

This is a wide, attractive set of stairs, fitted with handrails but not lights, rising over multiple landings along another of the city's walk-streets. Climb up 127 steps, admiring the nice homes on both sides and the impressive vegetable garden on the right as you go. (The last time I passed, it featured a bumper crop of Brussels sprouts!)

Land at the top at the cul-de-sac end of Granada, and continue walking straight ahead as the road rises and crests. At the next corner, stop and admire the very beautiful Craftsman structure on the left. It's a 1907 home, built by architect Edward Symonds, and is significant enough to have been named Historic-Cultural Monument No. 554 by the City of Los Angeles.

Note also, standing in the middle of Granada, looking south, the huge Eldred wooden staircase rising on the hillside across the canyon. This is the monster climb from Walk #7.

Turn right onto N. Avenue 53, and begin your ascent. On your right is another impressive freestone rock wall, and a good-looking iron gate behind it, on which you can see the names of the original tenants and the street address actually *stamped* into the concrete staircase. Continue past this, winding up and around, to the corner of Avenue 53 and Abbott Place. There are two grand old homes here, one on each corner, both with fittingly grand views east into the hills and north across the valley.

Continue up and over and down, along Avenue 53. At the first corner, turn right onto Aldama Street. Walk along, past Aldama Terrace, admiring the big old home at 5336, and past the turning for Umbria Street. At the bottom of the hill, turn left onto Avenue 54.

The houses are just as substantial here, but desperately in need of help. Mourn them, and walk along until the turning for Raphael Street. Turn left, walk up a half-block of roadway, then find your next staircase.

It's a sad one—27 steps up through graffiti, trash, unswept leaves, broken bottles, often a supermarket shopping cart or two, and a braying pit bull on one side. It's the staircase that time forgot, filthy and forsaken. Climb out of it, and walk straight ahead on Raphael.

Turn left, one block on, onto Aldama Terrace. Here, the ugly memory of the last staircase may be evaporated by the wondrous plaster Stonehenge construction in front of the lovely Craftsman at 619—mysterious, like the druid original, and smaller, but just as marvelous. Turn right, at the corner, back onto Aldama St. Walk straight ahead, following this road as it crosses Avenue 53 and bends to the left, passing several very good old homes and finally meeting Avenue 52.

Here, after a glance at the fine old Craftsman at 469 Avenue 52, now a group home run by Beacon Community Housing, turn left and head downhill. Just after the big green house at 432, beneath the sign indicating Abbott Place, look for a driveway leading to a staircase. And up! This is a newish, double-railed set of 56 steps, over several landings, in good condition, but not very well maintained, which will carry you up and onto the bend where Avenue 51 meets Shipley Glen Drive. Walk straight ahead, going down Shipley Glen.

Here you face the northern side of Mt. Washington. High up and to your right is the sweep of terraced boulevard where San Rafael Avenue heads for the Self-Realization Fellowship center, which you might have enjoyed on Walk #5. Straight ahead, too, is another look at those awesome Eldred steps.

At the bottom of the hill, Shipley Glen meets Avenue 50. Turn right, and—if it's open—pause to observe a Los Angeles rarity. Here, running under Avenue 50, serving the Aldama Elementary School, is a pedestrian *underpass*. It drops down 17 steps, runs under the street, and then climbs 18 steps back up the other side. The city used to have dozens of these, wherever elementary schools sat next to busy boulevards. Nowadays, most of them are closed. This one is still in use.

After you've enjoyed that, continue up the east side of Avenue 50 a short distance farther. Just before the big apartment building at 701, across from a signpost for Salient Drive, turn right and head uphill on your final staircase.

This is a roughly hewn piece of work, mostly unshaded, mostly unkempt, with a handrail, that rises 132 steps over multiple landings—the last of them uneven and slanting sideways. Land at 5037 Montezuma Street, turn left, and head uphill.

Montezuma bends right and flattens out, exposing some fine old Craftsman houses in varying stages of preservation and restoration. There are good hilltop views here of the San Gabriels to the north and west, and to Highland Park and Ernest Debs Regional Park to the south and east. You may also catch sight of a rare papaya tree, fruit bearing and beautiful, at 5075.

Montezuma becomes Aldama, and Aldama flattens out to meet Avenue 53. Turn right here and head uphill, admiring the sturdy old homes along the way, including the very charming cottage at 510 and its big brother next door. Crest the hill, passing the other side of Abbott Place again, and head down. Just below the point where Avenue 53 meets Granada, watch for a button hook right turn, onto the lower portion of Avenue 53. Take this down and around the strangely marooned palm tree in the cul-de-sac, and continue your descent. As the road flattens, there are significant structures at 330 and 326—a 1905 Craftsman officially known as Piper House, designated Historic-Cultural Monument No. 540—and across the street at 329. The block reeks of early Los Angeles lore.

Cross Monte Vista once more, and Marmion and the Gold Line tracks. Continue to Figueroa, and your starting point.

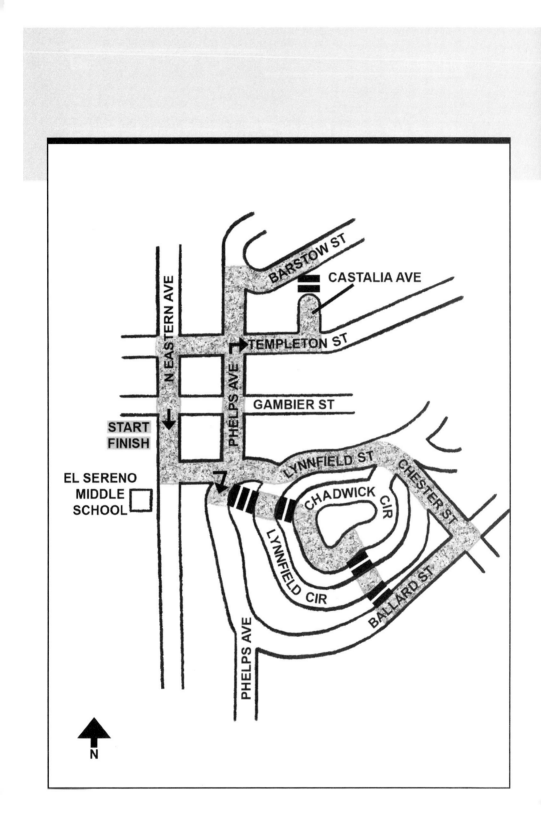

EL SERENO CIRCLES
DURATION: **40 minutes**
DISTANCE: **1.8 miles**
STEPS: **350**
DIFFICULTY: **3**
BUS: **#256**

This is a snappy walk through a seldom-visited section of the city; a compact walk that takes in a lot of elevation over a small amount of geography. Along the way are vast views of the San Gabriels and more barking dogs than you can shake a stick at.

Begin your walk along N. Eastern Avenue near the corner of Gambier Street, just south of Huntington Drive, maybe with a snack from the Tamale Man or Betty's Burgers—two longtime local favorites. Then head south on Eastern, with the beautiful El Sereno Middle School building on your right, and turn left onto Lynnfield Street. At the first corner, turn right onto Phelps Avenue. Just after the house at 2852, find the first staircase, to your left.

Like many of the staircases in the El Sereno area, this one is painted green—stairs, risers, handrail, and all. Climb up this relatively steep section of 83 stairs, over multiple landings, to Lynnfield Circle. You might be able to get a view here of Huntington Drive. In the early 1900s, a Pacific Electric Railway line ran up what is now Huntington's wide median strip. The railway was designed to link Downtown Los Angeles with the wealthy eastern communities of Pasadena and San Marino, but it also served the working-class community out of El Sereno.

Cross the road, and take the next staircase directly in front of you. Climb this one 99 steps, and land at 2746 Chadwick Circle. The views are grand from here. Depending on the marine layer and the winds, you can see far into the San Gabriel mountain chain, across Pasadena, Montecito Heights, and the Monterey Hills. Mt. Wilson's communications towers blink high above. In winter, the peaks are snow-capped and inviting.

Not so inviting are the dogs of El Sereno. You may have been yapped at coming up the Phelps-Lynnfield stairs. You will be similarly greeted at the next staircase. Turn right along Chadwick, heading counter-clockwise around the circle, picking up substantial southern views as you go. After a wide clearing over a steep drop to the right, and just before the house at 2802, find your next staircase.

This is a straight shot of 95 steps—without a landing, but with handrails and lights, and more barking dogs—installed in 1926 by the firm of J & P Cristich, and approved by Inspector W.F. Hile. At the bottom, walk directly across Lynnfield Circle, and catch the next set of stairs going down. This staircase is fitted again with lights and a rail, and drops 73 steps down to drop you at 2805 Ballard St. Turn left, and walk one long, flat block to the corner of Chester Street.

This must be the doggiest neighborhood in Los Angeles. Between the first pair of stairs, the second, and this block of Ballard St., I noted pit bulls, boxers, a snarling German shepherd, several nasty chows and a pack of snapping chihuahuas. They were all behind fences, and they were all very unfriendly.

Turn left and climb up Chester, greeting first Lynnfield Circle and then Chadwick Circle on your left. At the peak of the hill, bear left onto Lynnfield Street, and begin your descent. Again you are treated to fine views here, over the El Sereno flats and into the mountains beyond. Bear right, staying on Lynnfield, where the other side of Lynnfield Circle slips in, and at the bottom of the slope turn right onto Phelps Ave. Go straight for two blocks, and turn right onto Templeton Street.

This is an older, calmer neighborhood, dense with small, subdued bungalows and populated by fewer snarling dogs and more smiling people. Walk a length of Templeton, and at the first opportunity turn left, onto Castalia Avenue. At the end of the block, find your final staircase—a short sweep of 19 steps, fitted with a handrail, past one final barking hound. Turn left and head downhill along Barstow Street. At the next corner, turn left onto Phelps, once more. Pay particular attention to the charming bungalow courtyard on the right—a grand example of affordable single-family homes from the early 1900s.

Turn right onto Templeton. At the intersection, turn left onto Eastern, and you will be back at your starting point.

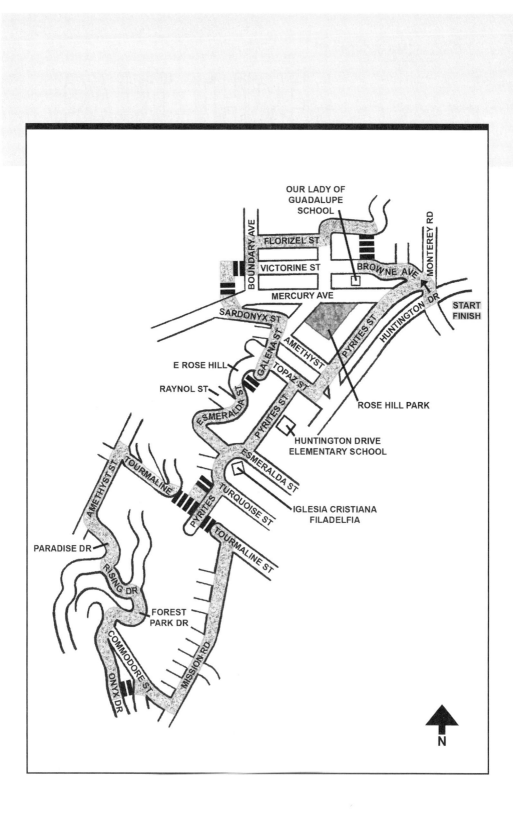

WALK #10

HAPPY VALLEY AND MONTECITO HEIGHTS
DURATION: **1 hour, 30 minutes**
DISTANCE: **3.7 miles**
STEPS: **626**
DIFFICULTY: **5**
BUS: **#78, 79, 378, 252**

*This is an astonishing walk—very long and very rigorous—
through one of the city's most unknown areas. As you walk
you'll find horizon-to-horizon views of the Los Angeles basin,
streets named after minerals and gemstones, and a network
of unpaved mountain roads—all less than five miles from City
Hall.*

Begin your walk near the intersection of Huntington Drive
and Monterey Road, perhaps with a snack from the Fresco Market or the Mr. Good's Donuts. Leave the intersection heading
west, and begin walking up Browne Avenue, past the big cross
marking Our Lady of Guadalupe and its Rose Hills school.

Browne rises slightly, passing the schoolyard below. Just
past 4537 is your first staircase. This is a C.R. Snow production
from 1928—curiously with different inspector stamps at the top
and bottom, and without lights or handrails—climbing 103 steps
to land at 4534 Florizel Street. Take a left, and head downhill. At
the bottom you will find Rose Hill Park on your right and low-
income government housing on your left. Walk between the two,
crossing Mc Kenzie Avenue and staying on Florizel, to the top of
the next rise. Here Florizel meets Boundary Avenue. Turn left,

walk a block, and find the next staircase on your right.

This is a recently constructed set of 27 steps that rises to a dirt road and goes . . . nowhere. The road up to the right leads to hiking trails in the park. The road down and to the left leads into a rather pleasant garden of drought-resistant native plants. Follow the downhill path as it bends to the right. On your left, you will see the next staircase, another new one, with 22 wide steps dropping down to Mercury Avenue.

Cross Mercury and turn left right away onto the oddly named Sardonyx Street. Walk a block's length of yappy dogs and chain-link fence, as the road wraps around the hillside and, at the stop sign, turns into Galena Street. Walk straight on, crossing Amethyst Street—the first of many gemstone or mineral streets you'll meet on this walk. Follow Galena as it drops down and around, and swing to the right as it meets N. Topaz Street. Bear to the right, and after one more block of Galena, find your next staircase.

This is more like it—a towering rise of 106 steps up a true walk-street, and again the work of C.R. Snow from 1928. There are lights and handrails, a fair amount of graffiti, and more yappy dogs. At the top, walk straight ahead. You are now on East Rose Hill Drive. Walk on, past the turning for Raynol Street—with its strange marooned island of a single palm—as East Rose Hill turns into Esmeralda Street and begins to descend.

The neighborhood takes on a distinctly rural feel here. You will see and hear roosters, and even geese, mixed in with the barking dogs. The views are grand. Across Huntington Dr. is the other side of Happy Valley, and behind it, the peak separating you from El Sereno. To the right are the steep hillsides dotted with pepper, eucalyptus, and palm, separating you from Montecito Heights. (During the fall, this hillside and many others on this walk will be covered with wild melons, too.) Walk straight on, as Esmeralda descends. Stop at the T-intersection with Pyrites Street, just before you bump into the Iglesia Cristiana Filadelfia, and just after admiring the stone garage and stairs behind 4360. Turn right onto Pyrites, and walk a block, past the turning for Turquoise Street. Here on the right, you will find the next set of stairs.

This is a grouping of 22 steps, climbing up to a raised sidewalk serving the uphill side of Pyrites. Follow the elevated walkway to its terminus. Here on the left, you will find more steps going back down to the roadway, and more steps beneath that going down to another street. Ignore these, and instead turn right and uphill, and take a sharp climb—up a narrow staircase, with multiple landings fitted with heavy-gauge handrails and overhead lighting, rising an impressive 191 steps to the top.

Catch your breath. Admire the view. Then continue uphill, onto the broken asphalt stretch of Tourmaline Street. After 50 feet or so, bear left onto an entirely unpaved section of Tourmaline. Now the road gets very steep, dusty, and rutted. Press on, climbing and climbing, past a couple of modest houses served by this messy piece of road, to the intersection with, again, Amethyst. Turn left, and walk a block.

At the turning for another unpaved road, this time another piece of Turquoise, take a small break. Turn right, and walk 50 feet. Far below you is the community of Montecito Heights. Directly in front of you is Downtown, as you've probably never seen it before. This is one of the best and most unusual views of the city skyline, and well worth a small detour. (It's difficult to believe, but this steep, unpaved, rutted, and ruined piece of roadway, despite the posted "No Through Street" sign, actually goes all the way to the bottom of the hill you're standing on. I've walked it. It must be the single most treacherous piece of city street anywhere in Los Angeles. Even a four-wheel drive vehicle, under ideal conditions, would have difficulty navigating it.)

Back on Amethyst, turn right and head south. Follow this as it descends a little, exposing westerly views of Dodger Stadium, Elysian Park, the Griffith Observatory, and the Hollywood sign. At the turning for Paradise Drive, if the gate further ahead is open, you can get even bigger views by bearing right and walking another 200 yards onto the roughly paved road there. If not, turn left onto Paradise, and begin your descent, along a stretch of bucolic, birdsy, shady hillside. Take the hard left onto Rising Drive, as Paradise continues around the hills, and then take the hard right onto Forest Park Drive.

The descent is sharper now. Far above, you can see Paradise and far below, Huntington. Follow Forest Park to the notch in the hill, and then turn left onto Commodore Street. Walk a block and turn right onto Onyx Drive. The poverty and neglect are deeper here. (One breezy day, I got hit by a tumbleweed coming right down the center of the street.) Admire the freestone fireplace down below, and the retaining walls made of concrete cylinders. Then, just across the street from 2601, find the next staircase heading down.

This is a deeply shaded J & P Cristich construction, undated, with partial handrails, dropping down 123 steps, between dogs competing for your attention. At the bottom, landing at a Y-intersection of Commodore and Mallard Street, cross the intersection and turn right, heading downhill on Commodore until you meet Mission.

Turn left. Walk along an ugly stretch of road, past the turning for Superior Court, and stay to the left as you approach the complicated over-under intersection of Mission, Huntington and N. Soto Street. Walk on, past Canto Drive, Moonstone Drive, and Radium Drive, and then turn left onto yet another section of Tourmaline. Up a very steep stretch of this block, past some period cottages, find your final staircase. Climb up 32 steps onto Pyrites, and turn right and head downhill.

Follow Pyrites all along, bearing left at the intersection with Turquoise, curving right past West Rose Hill and Esmeralda, past the Iglesia Cristiana Filadelfia, then turning left at the elementary school—always staying on Pyrites. The road rises up here, paralleling Huntington, above the schoolyard. Where it meets Topaz, turn right, then left again, and continue on Pyrites. You may notice some extremely old frame houses as you go along, some more than a hundred years old. (I particularly like the two shotgun-shack bungalows at the corner of Pyrites and Yorba.)

Ahead, you will see the large cross marking Our Lady of Guadalupe. Here you will find your beginning, and your end.

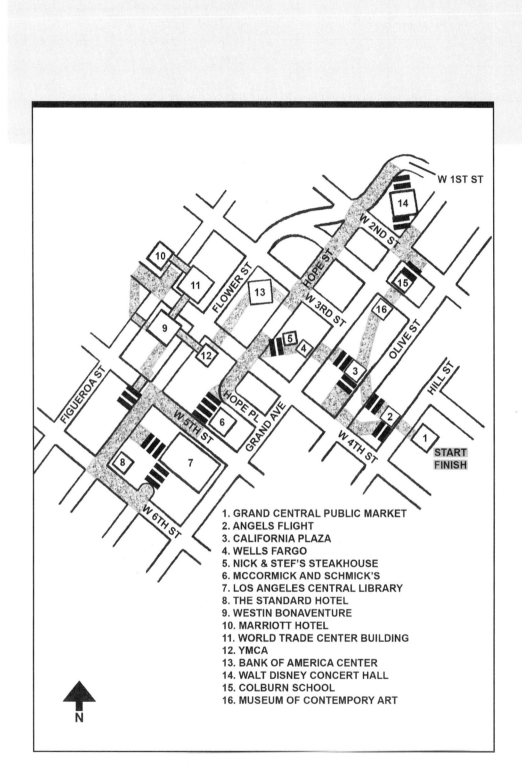

W 1ST ST

W 2ND ST

14

FLOWER ST

HOPE ST

13

W 3RD ST

10

11

15

9

16

5

12

4

OLIVE ST

3

HILL ST

FIGUEROA ST

HOPE PL

6

2

GRAND AVE

1

W 5TH ST

START
FINISH

8

7

W 4TH ST

W 6TH ST

1. GRAND CENTRAL PUBLIC MARKET
2. ANGELS FLIGHT
3. CALIFORNIA PLAZA
4. WELLS FARGO
5. NICK & STEF'S STEAKHOUSE
6. MCCORMICK AND SCHMICK'S
7. LOS ANGELES CENTRAL LIBRARY
8. THE STANDARD HOTEL
9. WESTIN BONAVENTURE
10. MARRIOTT HOTEL
11. WORLD TRADE CENTER BUILDING
12. YMCA
13. BANK OF AMERICA CENTER
14. WALT DISNEY CONCERT HALL
15. COLBURN SCHOOL
16. MUSEUM OF CONTEMPORY ART

N

WALK #11

DOWNTOWN LOS ANGELES
DURATION: **1 hour, 30 minutes**
DISTANCE: **3 miles**
STEPS: **1,021**
DIFFICULTY: **5**
BUS: **#2, 4, 10, 28, 81, 83, 90, 91
94, 302, 728, 794**

This is a fine urban walk through the very heart of the city, a massive hike that employs old staircases, new staircases, private staircases, and even circular staircases. Along the way are the city's only funicular railway, some of its finest public buildings, and some amusing "pedway" overpasses.

Begin your walk on N. Hill Street, midway between 3rd Street and 4th Street, perhaps with a Mexican or Chinese meal inside the wonderful Grand Central Public Market. When you've digested, cross Hill St. to the base of Angels Flight.

This is a great piece of Los Angeles history. Built in 1901 with funding from a contemporary of Abraham Lincoln, the two-track funicular rail system carried passengers up the steep slope to the top of Bunker Hill. It functioned without a hitch for 68 years, when it was dismantled in 1969 to make way for the great Bunker Hill renovation project. (If you've ever visited Heritage Square, off the Pasadena Freeway, that's where many of the great Bunker Hill Victorian houses went—moved whole, and transplanted in the Arroyo Seco.) The funicular was mothballed for 27 years, then restored and reopened with great ceremony.

Then, in 2001, one of the cars slipped its brakes. An 83-year-old passenger was killed, and Angels Flight was closed. For the past several years, the announcements of its "imminent" reopening have been a staple of Downtown gossip.

Luckily, however, the renovation designers included a staircase running beside the railway. Take these, and climb 121 steps to the top. Once there, turn and head across the little patch of green to your left. As you go, notice the *trompe l'oeil* portrait of window cleaners on the building high up to your left.

Walk through the gates at the end of the park, and cross S. Olive Street at the crosswalk. Once across, turn right and get the next set of stairs, a set that starts outdoors and ends indoors. Walk up a total of 85 stairs until you land on California Plaza's water garden level.

Here, you will find a panoply of coffee and lunch choices, as well as a sprinkling of humanity enjoying the wide-open spaces. Cross the plaza, staying to your left. On the other side, climb an additional 17 steps to the street level. Cross Grand Avenue now, and step up four stairs into the Wells Fargo plaza on the opposite side. Admire the large sculpture there, but keep walking straight on, toward Nick and Stef's Steakhouse. Drop down 21 steps, heading off to your left, and walk to Hope Street.

Go straight on Hope, toward 4th St. You're on top of Bunker Hill now, walking the landscape where Raymond Chandler, John Fante, and others set many of their most dramatic 1930s and 1940s stories. Almost nothing is left of that landscape except the views.

Straight ahead, cross 4th St. and continue on Hope as it begins to slope downhill. A block on, Hope will bend to the left. Walk straight on, toward the front doors of McCormick & Schmick's seafood restaurant. Climb five steps up, jog to the right, and take the delightful Bunker Hill steps going down— all 101 of them—taking in the fantastic views of the Los Angeles Central Library as you go.

This may be the quintessential Downtown Los Angeles structure—a 1926 design from Bertram Grosvenor Goodhue, who intended its tiled, mosaic pyramid tower, festooned with suns, sphinxes and snakes, to invoke the learned civilization of ancient Egypt. The building underwent a vast expansion and re-modeling during the 1980s, which fortunately left the original design relatively undisturbed.

Cross 5th Street, at the bottom of the Bunker Hill steps, turn right, and walk in the library's shadow, following its pe-rimeter to the corner of Flower Street. Turn left, and then turn left again into the library's front yard. Here, up an additional 16 steps, you get a fine view of the building and a tour of its gardens. Near the front door, follow the sidewalk around the right side of the building, then turn left through the gates and find the next collection of staircases going down—ultimately dropping 41 steps and landing once more on Hope. (Note here the constel-lation of "stars" in the street. Note also, up ahead a block or so, Library Bar, which drinkers say is a fine place to hoist a few.)

Walk a block down Hope, and turn right onto 6th St., passing The Standard hotel on your right. Cross Flower at the corner, and turn right, admiring the brightly colored staircases to nowhere in the middle of the fountain on your left in City Na-tional Plaza.

Just before you reach the corner, find the staircase rising up ahead of you. These steps lift you up and over 5th St., climb-ing 42 steps to the pedestrian overpass and dropping you on the other side. Now find the interior staircase going up on the right side. Take these two flights up for a total of 42 steps, and land on the plaza level high above 5th and Flower.

This broad open space is part of the sprawling Westin Bonaventure property. Off to the left you'll see their swimming pool. To the right is a beer hall and restaurant. Walk straight across the plaza between the two, in a westerly direction, to-ward signs for the "pedway." This delightful footpath-overpass will carry you across Figueroa Street, and deposit you in another wide, open plaza. Walk up and to your right, across the plaza, past the duck pond, to the far upper right-hand corner of the prop-erty. There, you will find a sidewalk leading you to 4th St. Turn right, and head downhill half a block to Figueroa. Cross 4th St. to your left, and head north on Figueroa. Turn in at the first drive-way, and walk through the front doors of the Marriott Hotel.

Through the lobby you will find, straight ahead, the es-calator to the second floor. (I'm sorry! It's not a staircase. If you like, try and walk the escalator up. If you hustle, you can squeeze 19 steps in before you land.) At the top, walk straight ahead, turn left and go around the side of the second floor lobby, and then left again, following the signs for the "pedway." Heading out of the building, you'll find a welcome water fountain and restroom on the left.

After your pit stop, exit the Marriott via the pedway and cross Figueroa once more. On the other side, you will enter the World Trade Center building. It is possible to turn left here, walk to the end of the building, and connect to a rather interesting covered walkway that goes on for blocks. For now, though, turn right instead and head up another escalator. (I'm sorry! It's not a staircase. But if you run up the "down" escalator, which is *not* recommended, you can squeeze 17 steps out of this staircase.) Exit the World Trade Center building, cross a little plaza, and enter the Westin Bonaventure.

Here things get a little tricky, but only a little. Walk to the right, once you enter. You are on the Bonaventure's 6th floor. As you walk, watch for a circular staircase on your left. Take these at the first opportunity, dropping down and around 26 steps, then 26 steps, then 26 more, until you have landed on the 3rd floor. Then walk straight ahead, through the very heart of the lovely circular building.

You'll find you are on the hotel's gymnasium level. Cafes, restaurants, sitting areas, the reception desk, and all the other accoutrements of a great city hotel are on the floors and land-ings above and below. All around you currently, however, is the hotel gym. Cross the running track, admiring the gleaming ex-ercise machines to the left and right, then find another circular staircase on the opposite side. Climb up, 26 steps and 26 steps and 26 steps, to reclaim the 6th floor. Then turn left, following the interior wall of the vaulted lobby, and turning right, heading out of the building, onto one final pedway.

This one crosses Flower, heading for the large, green YMCA building. Bear left, along the north side of the Y, continuing to the next corner. Here, cross 4th St. to your left, and then turn left and into the fine Bank of America Center gardens. (There is a farmer's market here on Friday mornings, from 11:00 AM to 2:00 PM.) Wind around the gardens, and around the back of the Bank of America building. Find your way back to Hope St., cross the street and turn left, heading north toward the Walt Disney Concert Hall.

It's several blocks away, but you will see it gleaming well before you arrive. The fantastical Frank Gehry building, an undulating mountain clad in shiny stainless steel skin, was a gift from Lillian Disney as a tribute to her late husband Walt. Years in the making, the hall opened in 2003 to rave reviews from everyone except the apartment-dwellers across Hope St.—they were blinded by the late afternoon sun reflecting off the hall's shiny exterior. One entire wing of the building was ultimately buffed down to a matte finish to preserve peace on Bunker Hill.

Stay on Hope as you cross 2nd St. and approach 1st Street. There, at the corner, make a hairpin right turn onto the Disney property, taking the wide marble staircase up 41 steps to the garden level. Just ahead and to your left, stop and admire the rose-shaped Delft china fountain. The "A Rose for Lilly" sculpture, a gift from Gehry to his benefactor, is allegedly the result of Lillian's distaste for the huge collection of blue-and-white crockery she'd been given over the decades by people who mistakenly thought it pleased her. Gehry had hundreds of Delftware porcelain vases and tiles broken and pasted into a rose-shaped fountain form. True or not, an amusing story.

Slide past this, bending left with the contour of the building, ultimately finding your way to another wide marble staircase heading down. Drop 69 steps down to land on Grand Avenue. Take a left, go to the corner, and cross Grand. Take a right and cross 2nd St. Turn left, heading downhill, and catch the staircase on the left taking you up 24 steps onto the plaza outside the Colburn School, a performing arts academy and music conservatory. Walk past this, dead ahead, along the back entrance to the Museum of Contemporary Art. Shortly after, you will find yourself once more in the water garden of the California Plaza. Wind around to your left, past the spraying fountains. You'll see the top of Angels Flight on your left. Keep going. Bear right, and find the 36-step staircase carrying you down to the lower level. Take a buttonhook right, and take the penultimate sets of stairs down 32 steps to land at the top of the Angels Flight staircase.

Walk down, walk down, dropping down the 121 steps to regain Hill St., Grand Central Market, and your starting point.

PART TWO

ECHO PARK

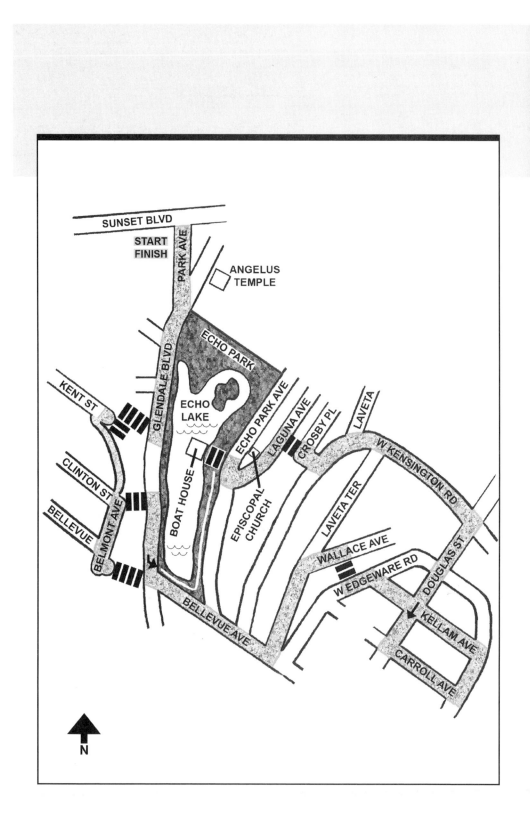

ECHO PARK LAKE VICTORIANS
DURATION: **1 hour, 15 minutes**
DISTANCE: **3 miles**
STEPS: **428**
DIFFICULTY: **2.5**
BUS: **#2, 4**

This is a mostly flat walk past venerable Echo Park Lake and through Angelino Heights, home of the city's oldest Victorian and Queen Anne mansions. It includes panoramic views of Downtown and a lot of Los Angeles history.

Begin your walk near the corner of Sunset Boulevard and N. Alvarado Street, perhaps with a meal at Alexander's Brite Spot, a cheery coffee shop and hipster hangout just east of there. When you are satisfied, walk south from Sunset on Park Avenue, heading toward Echo Park Lake.

Going down the slope, you will begin to get views of the lake, and of the massive Angelus Temple to your left. This was the headquarters of 1920s evangelist Aimee Semple McPherson, and her Foursquare Church, and continues to draw thousands to its Sunday services.

Bear right as Park meets Glendale Boulevard, and head south. Across the street, you will see the statue of Jose Marti, hero of Cuba's independence from Spain. I'm not sure why he's in Echo Park, but it's a fine statue. Near him is the end of the lake traditionally reserved for the park's annual Lotus Festival. In recent years, the lotuses have died out. The festival continues, but without its signature blossom.

Continue on Glendale, past Santa Ynez Street and the very impressive Spanish Colonial Revival-style home at 817. It is said to be a 1937 construction from architect John Victor Macka, and seems incongruous on this busy boulevard.

Just ahead, at the signpost indicating Kent Street, find your first staircase going up. This is a massive old mountain of poured concrete, usually decorated with murals, with rails and lights. It rises 28 steps, hits a walkway, and rises 12 more before turning into sidewalk and running along under some huge old date palms. Just past the house number for 1715, find your next staircase, rising up 26 steps on the left. This will deposit you at the end of Kent St. Turn left, and head downhill as Kent ends and turns into a wide sidewalk. Follow the sidewalk, bordered by a gray-white fence, as it curves around the contour of the hill.

The views here are magnificent. Below you is the lake, with its towering fountain and Victorian-era boathouse. Behind the lake, you can see the dark brown Protestant Episcopal Church at the lake's edge. Far up and to the left, you can see the gleaming domes of St. Andrew's Ukrainian Orthodox Church. As you wind along the pathway, you will see City Hall and the Downtown skyline.

You will also see a lot of graffiti, beer bottles, and cigarette butts—indicators that this is perhaps not a good place to be at night.

At the end of the walkway, you meet Clinton Street. Bear left, and find your next staircase, this time going down. This is another massive structure, a twin-sided beauty, adorned with heavy chains, stylish in construction, and in dire need of a paint job. It drops down, with handrails but no lighting, 88 steps. Follow these down to Glendale Blvd. and turn right, heading south once more.

At the corner of Bellevue Avenue, cross Glendale with the light, walk down into the park itself, and follow the pathway to your right, going counter-clockwise around the lake. Here, the street noise abates somewhat. Overhead is a surprising selection of palms—date palms, royal palms, Florida palms, Washingtonia palms, and more. Enjoy the shade and the sight of joggers, dog walkers, elderly Tai Chi practitioners, remote-control boat captains, and the other citizens enjoying their park.

As you approach the boathouse, which is the tired but elegant building at the water's edge on your left, watch for the staircase going up to the right. Take these 12 steps up to Echo Park Avenue. Cross at the crosswalk, directly in front of you, and bear left onto Laguna Avenue.

Follow Laguna for a long half-block, crossing behind the Episcopal church you saw from above the lake. Just past the house at 946, take the next staircase—a series of 84 steps, a slightly shabby set, with handrails and graffiti, but without lights—which lifts you from Laguna to Crosby Place. Walk up a steep quarter-block of Crosby, and turn left onto West Kensington Road.

You are now in Angelino Heights, a rather exclusive neighborhood that is home to the city's greatest collection of restored Victorian and Queen Anne homes. Kensington is the outermost ring of a series of circular streets. Walk along Kensington, past the two turnings for Laveta Terrace, enjoying the increasingly interesting homes as you go—in particular, the terrific cactus garden in front of the charming red bungalows at the second Laveta corner. Continue to Douglas Street, and turn right. Walk straight ahead, deeper into the heart of Angelino Heights, and turn left onto Carroll Avenue.

Here, you will find a concentration of beautifully restored period homes. All of them are marvelous, but particularly noteworthy are the stately Queen Annes and Victorians at 1344, 1330, 1320, 1316, and the massive corner house at 1300. Notice the period lampposts and, here and there, the stone street-side carriage steps. These were designed to help passengers in and out of their high, horse-drawn cabriolets and phaetons. Some of these are accompanied by old wrought-iron hitching posts, too.

At the bottom of Carroll, turn left onto East Edgeware Road, pausing to observe the fine widow's walk on top of the Victorian-era home at 724. Go a block, and turn left onto Kellam

Avenue, noting here the old corner market, now turned into a residence. Along here you will see less-dramatic, less-restored versions of the period masterpieces, as well as some sturdy old Craftsman homes. Especially fine are the little bungalows at 1314 and 1320, and the bigger homes at 1343 and 1349. Crossing Douglas at the corner, don't miss the huge Mission Revival mansion at 1405.

Follow Kellam down to the corner of West Edgeware Road. Turn left, and cross the street. Just past the apartment building at 1092, find your next staircase going down. This is a wide, attractive staircase—a C.H. Johnston construction, undated—without rails or lights, running beside a large, red barn-like structure on the right. It drops down 57 steps to land on Wallace Avenue. Turn left onto Wallace, walk a short distance to the corner—pausing to admire the curved wooden staircase at 1495—and turn left again onto Laveta Terrace.

This is a low, flat street, running down toward the Hollywood Freeway. It is not without its charms, but they are less obvious than the Victorians of Angelino Heights. Near the corner, you will meet some very old, shingle-sided bungalows that look as if they haven't even been painted since their construction a hundred years ago.

Make a right at the corner, onto Bellevue, but first notice an oddity across the street. It looks like a staircase, but it is actually a pedestrian tunnel that runs *under* the Hollywood Freeway, connecting two ends of Laveta Terrace. It is quite a rarity. I know of only one other in Hollywood, a pedestrian extension of Lemon Grove Avenue near the intersection of Melrose and Normandie. (There are also several others, now closed, near the intersection of Magnolia Boulevard and Colfax Avenue, which once helped pedestrians cross under the 170 freeway to get to North Hollywood Park.)

Turn right onto Bellevue. Walk straight ahead two blocks to Echo Park Ave., trying to ignore the roar of the freeway, and one block more to Glendale. Cross with the light. Dead ahead you will find your next staircase. Note the period lamp globes as you climb up 55 zigzag steps over several landings, with hand-rails, to land on the sidewalk end of Bellevue. Walk on a short bit, shaded by palms and walnut trees, to the corner of Belmont Avenue.

    To the left, at the cul-de-sac end of Belmont, is another pedestrian peculiarity—a footpath *over* the Hollywood Freeway. Check this out, if you like, and then continue back the other way on Belmont, heading north. At the first corner, you will see the heavy chains marking the top of the Clinton stairs you took earlier. Walk on, back along the lake view sidewalk. Far up ahead, if the air is clear, you will see the concrete Garbutt House (featured in Walk #22) at the top of the hill separating Echo Park from Silver Lake. Press on. Turning back onto Kent St., drop down the 26 stairs to your right, turn right onto the walkway heading down, and descend the final sets of 12 and 28 steps to land again on Glendale. Turn left, walk to Park, turn left again, and find your way back to the starting point.

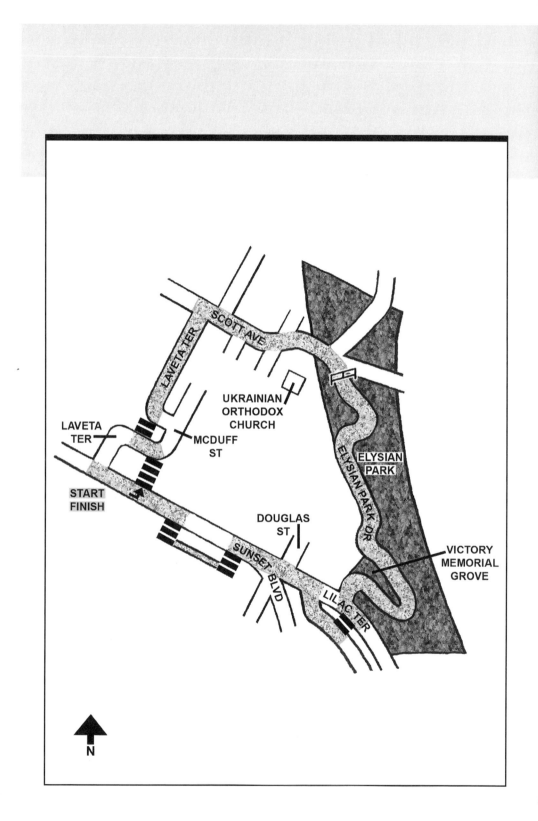

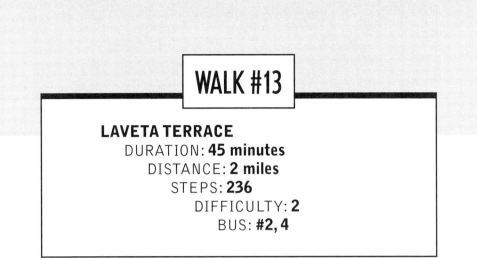

WALK #13

LAVETA TERRACE
DURATION: **45 minutes**
DISTANCE: **2 miles**
STEPS: **236**
DIFFICULTY: **2**
BUS: **#2, 4**

This is a relatively gentle Echo Park walk that takes in the neighborhood's most elegant staircase, sweeping views of Chavez Ravine and Downtown Los Angeles, a stroll through Elysian Park, and a look at hidden city streets.

Begin your walk on Sunset Boulevard, east of Echo Park Avenue, near the corner of Laveta Terrace, perhaps with a Mexican meal at the ancient Barragan's or a hipster breakfast at Lot 1 Café. Then walk east, on the north side of the street, to the corner of McDuff Street. Turn left into the parking lot, and find your first staircase.

This is an uneven, lop-sided set of 74 steps, with rails but no lights, that lifts you to the elbow at 1340 Laveta Terrace. Turn left and go downhill for half a block. There on the right, you'll come to Echo Park's most elegant set of stairs—a broad, wide staircase, bordered by attractive walls and benches, illuminated at night by graceful old streetlamps. Climb up the four flights of 64 steps to land again on Laveta Terrace.

Walk straight ahead, down a road lined with massive palms—some are 80 to 90 feet tall—planted almost a hundred years ago, spaced one every 20 feet. Notice a peculiar architectural feature as you go. Almost every home on the west side of the street is a two-story structure, and almost every home on the east side is a one-story structure.

Turn right at the first corner, onto Scott Avenue, and begin a gentle climb uphill toward Elysian Park. Up ahead and to the right you can see the golden spires of St. Andrew's Ukrainian Orthodox Church. (To see it in person, you can go later to the top of Sutherland Street, which comes off Sunset, east of Echo Park Ave.) You'll pass Sargent Place and Portia Street and, continuing on the right side of Scott, go into a shady bower of dracaena and oleander. When you emerge, you'll be at a three-way intersection. To the left is a pathway into Elysian Park. Straight ahead is the road into the park, toward Dodger Stadium. To the right is a blocked roadway. Take this turn, walking over or around the low white gate, onto the closed stretch of Elysian Park Drive.

The roadway is empty and quiet during the daytime, but shows signs of activity at night; the pavement itself is tagged with graffiti. Walk ahead, appreciating the coast live oaks, eucalyptus, and pepper trees on the hillside on your right, and the open views of Dodger Stadium to your left. Below is the Barlow Respiratory Hospital (formerly the Barlow Sanitarium), a privately held tuberculosis hospital for Los Angeles's poor, founded in 1902 by Walter Jarvis Barlow, who bought a 25-acre parcel of land from the well-known Los Angeles landowner J.B. Lankershim for $7,300. Dr. Barlow, who had come west looking for a dry climate to cure his own tuberculosis, would go on to help found the Los Angeles Philharmonic Orchestra and to act as dean of the UCLA School of Medicine.

Elysian Park Dr. will wind around and end at a set of metal gates. If you double back to your right, into the grove of pepper trees, you can get a good close view of the backside of the Ukrainian Church and its glorious golden spires. Otherwise, continue straight ahead, past the gates, and continue across the intersection, bearing left.

This length of road on a hot day is an oasis of shade and breeze, thick with trees and vines. There isn't much traffic here, because the roadway ahead is also gated and closed.

Just past those gates, on your left, you'll find a set of brick stairs on the left, nine steps leading up the foundation of what was once a large private home. All that's left now is a memorial stone to 21 fallen soldiers who "made the supreme sacrifice," a plaque reads, in the First World War. The plaque was placed by the Daughters of the American Revolution in 1921.

Just beyond the memorial, another set of eight bricked stairs returns you to the roadway. Turn left, and cruise downhill, alongside the Victory Memorial Grove below you. As the road hairpins back to the right, take a paved pathway to the left, under the trees and into the shade. Follow this pathway until it also hairpins back to the right, and follow that until the path meets the road again.

This is Lilac Terrace, a split roadway leading down to Elysian Park Avenue. Take a left, heading downhill. After about 75 feet, watch on the right side for a wooden staircase. With caution, take the 24 creaky old stairs to the downhill side of Lilac. Then turn right, and head back uphill. Lilac arches up and over and down, and lands at the corner of Sunset Blvd. and Douglas Street.

A stretch of busy, charmless Sunset lies before you. But even this is not without hidden delights. Cross Sunset at Douglas and continue walking west on Sunset. At the marking for number 1428, take what appears to be a set of private stairs, 13 in number, up to the left. Rise up two more steps, and follow the sidewalk leading to a half dozen very old houses. Climb seven more steps, and enter the deep shade thrown by the flowering magnolia, fruit-bearing fig, olive and avocado, bordered by flowering prickly pear and pungent salvia, all ending with a fine spreading palm. Take the sidewalk as it slopes and drops down another 35 very uneven steps and lands you back on Sunset. Straight ahead, you'll find your starting place.

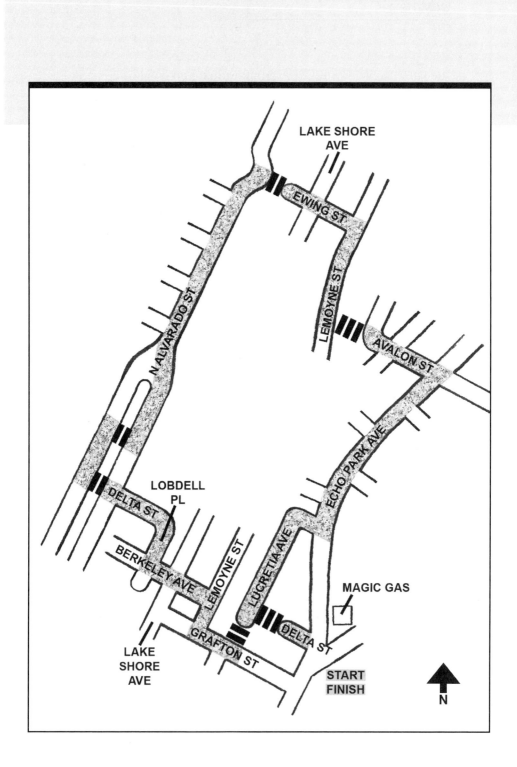

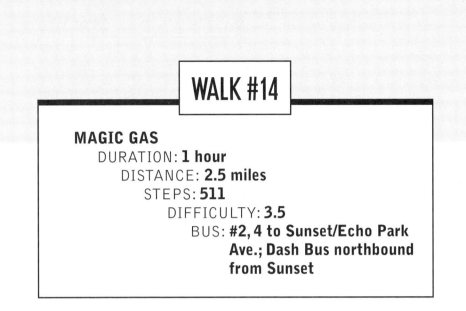

MAGIC GAS
DURATION: **1 hour**
DISTANCE: **2.5 miles**
STEPS: **511**
DIFFICULTY: **3.5**
BUS: **#2, 4 to Sunset/Echo Park Ave.; Dash Bus northbound from Sunset**

This is a rigorous walk up and down steep streets and even steeper staircases, with lots of elevation change and towering city views.

Find your way to the corner of Echo Park Avenue and Delta Street, near the Magic Gas service station. Obtain nutrients and coffee at Chango. Then walk a half-block up Delta to your first staircase. Climb 125 steps over multiple landings, with handrail but without lights, admiring the abundant agave cactus as you go.

Land at 1559 Lucretia Street, and turn right. Head downhill, noting the Dodger-themed art at 1637, as Lucretia curves to the right and hits Echo Park. Turn left, and walk three blocks to Avalon Street. Looking over and right, you'll see the massive Avalon stairs featured in Walk #15. No fear. Those aren't for today. Turn left onto Avalon instead, and walk straight ahead, up the slight slope to your next staircase.

Here you will find another 125 steps up, in several stages, without handrails but with lights, under some welcome shade.

This is another true walk-street, whose few houses are not served by any other roadway.

You emerge onto Lemoyne Street. Turn right, heading uphill, along a block of mixed architectural styles and underneath a profusion of aged fruit trees. Just past the house at 1943 and before the shiny-sided Tony Unruh-designed rectangle ahead, turn left and take the steep alley—it's actually a driveway-like length of Ewing Street—heading downhill. Take care. At the bottom, the alley is unpaved. When you've maneuvered across this, cross Lake Shore Avenue and find the next staircase, up another length of Ewing, straight ahead.

This is a steep set of 129 stairs, with rails on both sides but no lights, climbing up to N. Alvarado Street. Halfway up, enjoy the substantial views of Downtown Los Angeles. At the top, turn left and head downhill along Alvarado.

At the corner of Duane there are very good views to the right, across the gully to the Garbutt House (mentioned in Walk #22) and Hathaway Hill Estates. Straight ahead, you can see the stately old Queen of Angels Hospital. (It is now the headquarters of the Dream Center, an Assemblies of God mission whose pastor is also pastor of Sister Aimee's Angelus Temple.) Go down and down, following Alvarado, and then bear left to the uphill side as the boulevard splits.

Just down and to the right, off Glendale Boulevard, is a large public storage facility. It was once the home of Keystone Studios, operated by silent film star Mack Sennett. At the time of its construction in 1912, it was the first totally enclosed film studio in history.

Near the house at 1644, find the next staircase, heading down to the right. This will take you 37 steps over a zigzag pattern, and drop you on the lower half of Alvarado. Turn left, walk to the corner of Delta St., and take the zigzag staircase 31 steps up to your left. Then continue along Delta. At the corner, turn right into the alley-like Lobdell Place. Then turn left onto Berkeley Avenue.

Follow this across Lake Shore, past the preschool on

your right, and turn right onto Lemoyne St. After one block, turn left onto Grafton Street, and after one block more, as Lucretia comes in on your right, find the next staircase heading up to your left.

This is a steep, skinny, messy set of 64 steps, rising up through a depressing collection of rubbish, broken glass, and graffiti. There are handrails, but no lights, with lots of evidence of nighttime misbehavior and no evidence at all of oversight or maintenance. What a shame.

At the top, walk 50 feet into the cul-de-sac end of Lucretia, turn right and take the Delta stairs going back downhill. Drop down the 125 steps, walk the one block to Echo Park Ave. and your starting point.

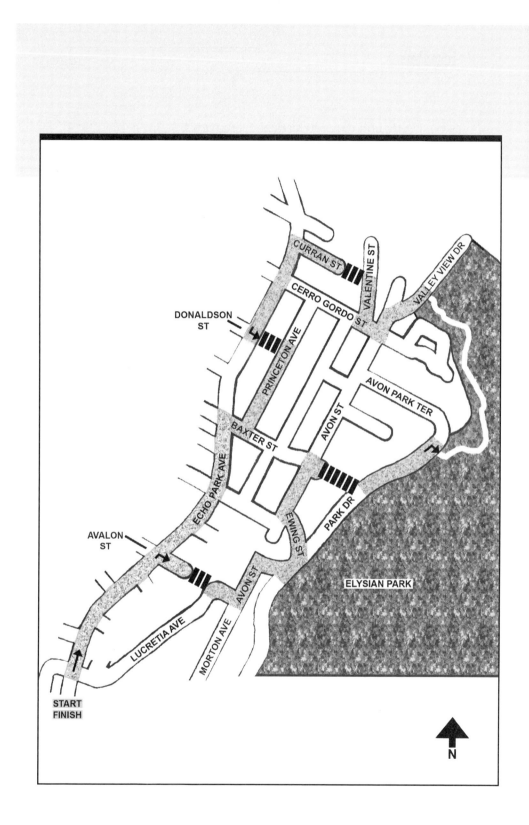

WALK #15

AVALON-BAXTER LOOP
DURATION: **1 hour, 30 minutes**
DISTANCE: **3.5 miles**
STEPS: **695**
DIFFICULTY: **4.5**
BUS: **#2, 4 to Sunset/Echo Park Ave.; Dash Bus northbound from Sunset**

This is Echo Park's most rigorous walk—the highest number of steps in the minimum amount of time—with a surplus of physical beauty. Along the way are views from Downtown to Westwood, a walk in Elysian Park, and a Who's Who of the historic Los Angeles arts scene and of the area's famous communists and socialists.

Begin your walk on Echo Park Avenue near the corner of Lucretia Avenue, perhaps with a pastry and coffee from the delightful Delilah Bakery on that corner, and then head north on Echo Park. Walk up past Effie Street, past the little grocery market called Little Grocery Market and, on the east side of the street, a series of artists' galleries. (If the gate is open, look for strange and wondrous metal sculptures within.) Just beyond, at Avalon Street, turn right, walk up a short, steep block, and meet your first staircase.

This is a recently reconstructed monster, steep and narrow, with handrails and lights, rising a staggering 192 steps across an open hillside where it's not uncommon to see coyotes, foxes, and even deer. Rise up, rise up, enjoying Echo Park's views behind you, including one of the parallel Avalon steps that run from Vestal Avenue to Lemoyne Street, and are part of Walk #14. At the top, take the gravel walkway to the street, and turn left onto Lucretia.

Down and to the right you will get a good view of lower Echo Park, including the domed roof of the Foursquare Church's Angelus Temple, the 5,300-seat hall where evangelist Aimee Semple McPherson began preaching the gospel in the 1920s.

After you've caught your breath, walk uphill on Lucretia, and turn left at the corner and proceed uphill on Avon Street. Climb up and over the little rise, under the shade of pepper trees on both sides of the street. Follow Avon as it bends to the right and meets Park Drive. Turn left onto Park.

Off to your right is Elysian Park, and, down below, Elysian Valley. To your left is a signpost for Duane Street—but there's no street. (More about this in a bit.) Walk straight on for a block, and take the left-hand turn onto Ewing Street. Follow this down, to a junction with another section of Avon, and turn right. This will take you up and over another rise, into deep eucalyptus shade. Down the other side, find the Baxter Street stairs on your right.

This is the big one—the largest set of steps in the Echo Park-Silver Lake-Franklin Hills area—with 231 risers, over multiple landings, lifting you up once more to Park Dr. At the top, as you catch your breath, enjoy the huge western views across Echo Park and into Silver Lake, Los Feliz, Griffith Park, and the Observatory, and to the Hollywood sign, Hollywood, the Sunset Strip and, finally, the towers of Century City and Westwood.

Walk to the road and turn left onto Park Dr., and enjoy a well-earned stretch of flat, peaceful roadway. To the right are views of Downtown and the hiking trails of Elysian Valley—well worth exploring. (There are also several large metal sculptures of birds hidden in the trees here, but I'm never able to find them without a local guide pointing them out.) To the left, as you walk along, are views of Glendale and Forest Lawn Memorial Park.

A little farther along, where Park Dr. bends to the left and turns into Avon Park Terrace, turn right onto the pathway into Elysian Park. (Don't go straight ahead, up the paved driveway. That's private property.) A few feet in, take the dirt road up and to the left, enjoying the shade and the profusion of oak, eucalyptus, palm, pine, and pepper trees. Where the trail appears to split, head left—but not before enjoying the overlook, with sweeping views of Mt. Washington, Glassell Park's Frogtown section, the Los Angeles River, and the Taylor Yard railway switching station.

Return to the dirt road, with the big water tower on your left. You may catch a glimpse of an old adobe home behind the water tower. It's one of the area's oldest homes—so old that the residents are permitted to stable horses here. Walking on, you may soon see (and smell) the horses themselves, up and to the left beside the water tank.

Continue as the dirt road begins to descend. After several hundred feet, as the descent becomes quite steep, watch for a narrow path leading off to the left. (If you come to a hard right-hand switchback, and a stone retaining wall, you've gone 200 feet too far.) Follow this path to the roadway ahead and turn left and downhill onto Valley View Drive. This will lead you down to another section of Avon. Turn left onto Avon, then immediately right onto Cerro Gordo Street, and then immediately right again onto Valentine Street. About 300 feet ahead you will find the next staircase, on your left side.

This is one of the city's best-maintained staircases, 129 steps up a walk-street with delightful cottages on both sides. (The contractor's stamp reads "Withers and Crites," and the inspector's stamp reads "G. Cake"—all of which sound like inventions of the Marx Brothers or the Three Stooges.) The staircase deposits you at the cul-de-sac end of West Curran Street. Walk over the crest and down the slope, admiring the fine wood frame houses as you go. At the bottom of the hill, turn left onto Echo Park Ave. once more.

This area was once known as "Red Hill," because it was

home to a profusion of left-leaning writers and artists. The folksinger and activist Woody Guthrie is said to have lived at the corner of Ewing and Preston Avenue. Writers Carey McWilliams and Upton Sinclair lived in the area, too. So did a host of key California artists, among them novelist John Fante and film director John Huston. The Eagles' Glenn Frey lived nearby, and so did Jackson Browne and Frank Zappa. Consider their contributions as you descend.

On the return route, you have choices. You could turn right, up Cerro Gordo, and do the first section of Walk #14. You could go straight, and continue on Echo Park, back to the starting point. Or you could include one more staircase. Go on! Turn left at the corner of Donaldson Street, and under the shade of the spreading pepper tree find your final climb.

This is a sharp rise up another walk-street, a hike of 143 stairs, fitted with rails and lights, carrying you from Echo Park to Princeton Avenue. Behind you, across the canyon, you can see the other set of Donaldson steps. Directly ahead, at the cul-de-sac end of Donaldson, is an overlook with good views of Elysian Park and a goat trail, not recommended for walking, back down to Valentine St.

Instead, turn downhill on Princeton, heading south, and enjoy one more quad-collapsing downhill descent. At the bottom, where Princeton meets Baxter, you can admire the Baxter stairs to your left, and then turn to Echo Park Ave. on your right. Turn left at the corner, and head back down Echo Park.

Slow and stop at the corner of Duane St., where an ancient sign in Japanese advertises some unknowable product or service. To the left, above the cul-de-sac end of Duane, you can see remnants of an old wooden staircase, which probably used to connect to the spot where the otherwise pointless Duane St. signpost sits on Park Dr. up above. The stairs are rotted out now and end in dust a dozen steps up.

Continue down Echo Park, past the turning for the Avalon stairs, past Effie, and back to Delilah and your starting point.

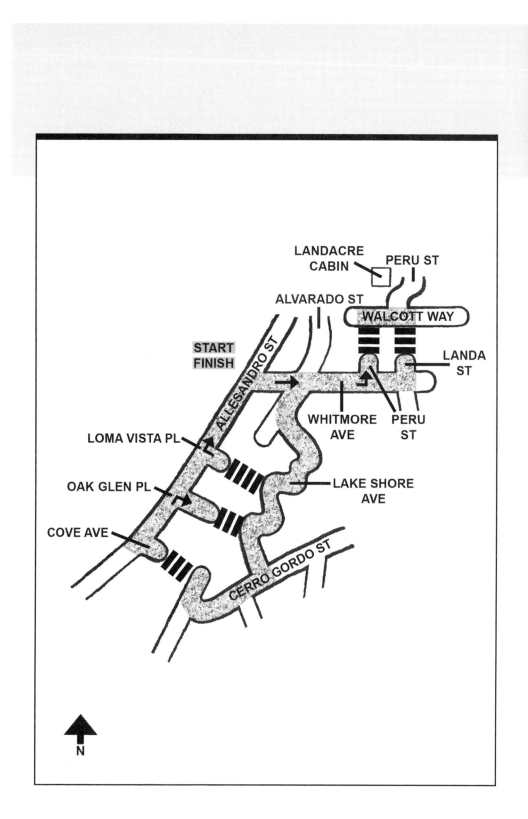

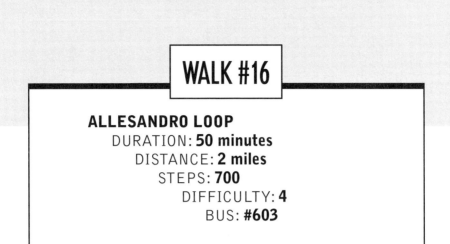

WALK #16

ALLESANDRO LOOP
DURATION: **50 minutes**
DISTANCE: **2 miles**
STEPS: **700**
DIFFICULTY: **4**
BUS: **#603**

This is a short, rigorous walk that takes in a lot of altitude. The charm of the walk-streets and the peculiarities of the neighborhood should compensate for the absence of a good café to start and stop from.

Start your walk on Allesandro Street, east of the Glendale Freeway and south of Riverside Drive. Park on the east side of the street, near the intersection with Whitmore Avenue. Walk up Whitmore, and after two blocks turn left onto Peru Street. Dead ahead: Your first staircase. Climb the 114 steps—lighted, but without handrails—up to Walcott Way, then turn right and walk to the corner.

Here, a short detour. To the left, Peru St. continues, heading downhill. Walk 100 yards and look down to your left. The Craftsman below you is the former home of Paul Landacre, considered during his lifetime to be America's premier wood engraver and linoleum block artist. Landacre lived in the ramshackle cabin from 1932 until his death in 1963. The house was named Historic-Cultural Monument No. 839 in 2006. You might also see the top of the Corralitas steps (featured in Walk #27) on the hillside beyond the Glendale Freeway. But that's a walk for another day.

Return to Walcott and turn left. A short distance up, find your next staircase on the right. This is a mirror of the Peru steps, going down a walk-street section of Landa Street, dropping 151 steps over nine landings, with lights but without handrails, a 1928 construction from the firm of Brockman, O'Brien, and Collins and bearing the mark of "Rumble City Inspector." At the bottom, walk the rest of Landa to the corner and turn right onto Whitmore Avenue.

One block down you pass Peru, and after another block, turn left onto N. Alvarado Street.

Climb up to the corner, and turn left onto Lake Shore Avenue. Follow this as it rises and bends to the right, enjoying the increasing shade as you go. Up the hill, to your left, you can see a number of homes hidden in the trees. Among them are some marvelous old Craftsman homes, the oldest of which was built in the early 1900s.

Continuing up, if you have sharp eyes, you will see a set of stairs on the right, just past the house at 2275. Ignore these and press on, appreciating the shady overhang of pepper and oak trees. If you have extra sharp eyes, you'll see another set of stairs just where Lake Shore meets Oak Glen Place. Ignore these too.

Instead, climb up a bit more, to the intersection with Cerro Gordo Street. Turn right. Walk along a welcome stretch of flat street, taking in a view of the Downtown skyline to the left, and continue to the end of Cerro Gordo. Here, at the T-intersection with Alvarado, you will get gigantic western views of the Moreno Highlands straight ahead, the Garbutt House and Hathaway Hill Estates slightly to the left, and Forest Lawn and Glendale up to the right. (A couple of blocks to the left is the section of Fargo Street where photographer William Claxton captured the iconic 1956 image of Echo Park resident Art Pepper, carrying his sax like a field hand heading for work.)

When you've had enough of the views, turn right on Alvarado, to the dead end just ahead. There you'll find the top of the Cove Avenue stairs.

This is a lovely group of stairs, dropping down 198 steps, with a handrail and lights, past a collection of beautiful old clapboard homes. The steps were built by M.W. McCombs, and are nicely accompanied by jade, dracaena, holly, walnut, and a couple of towering deodar cedar trees and, at the bottom, a fine Canary Island date palm. From the third landing, you can see a set of steps across the Glendale Freeway, but don't get excited. These used to serve the Red Car line that ran where the freeway now runs; the stairs themselves drop into a chain-link fence and a clump of bushes, but go nowhere.

At the bottom of the hill, you land at 2130 Cove. Walk to the corner and turn right. You're back on Allesandro. Go 100 yards, past the stop sign, and turn right onto Oak Glen Place.

This is one of the difficult sections. It's a short street, but it's *very* steep, and without much to recommend it but for a couple of fine palms and a garden of nice succulents. Turn around, as you go, and glimpse the Edendale steps climbing up the opposite hillside.

At the cul-de-sac top is one of the city's few remaining sets of wooden stairs. (According to history, all of the public stairs were originally made of wood. The cement staircases laid in the 1920s replaced the wooden staircases.) In this case, you've got 26 original wooden steps, followed by 32 cement ones.

At the top, turn left and head down the stretch of Lake Shore that you came up a while ago. Just after number 2255, at the end of the long redwood fence, turn left onto that section of steps you passed earlier.

This is a series of 39 very unsteady wooden steps that have a distinctly homemade feel to them. Watch yourself as you go—they could crumble at any time—and appreciate the painted fence to your left, adorned with primitive art and a hand-drawn sign that says "Por Favor No Tag."

After the stairs end, bend left down a stretch of unpaved path and watch your step here, too. The path is slippery, and lined by sharp-edged agave plants. At the end of the pathway, emerge onto the top of Loma Vista Place.

This is a charming block of old clapboard houses, well preserved and maintained, with a set of short, shallow steps running down the center of the road. Walk down 140 steps to the bottom of the cul-de-sac, where you'll find a chartreuse apartment building on one side and a mustard-colored house on the other. Turn right, back onto Allesandro, and walk the short distance back to Whitmore and your starting place.

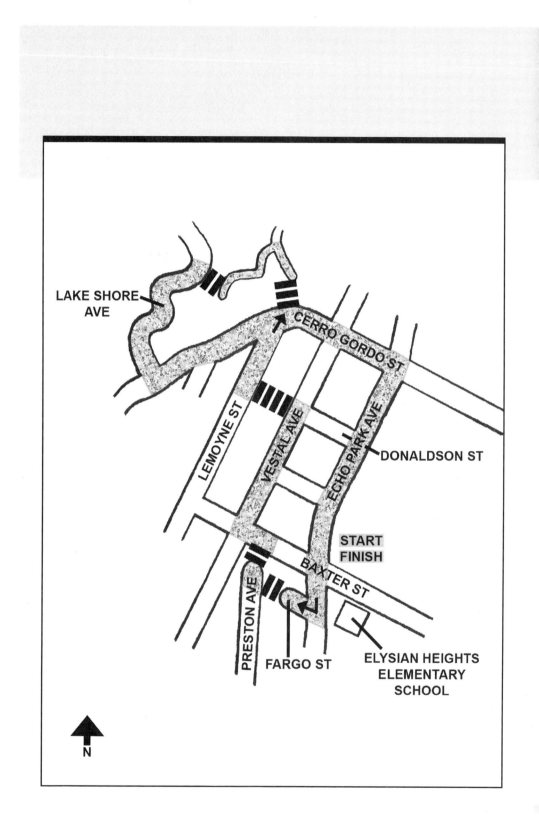

LAKE SHORE
AVE

CERRO GORDO ST

LEMOYNE ST

VESTAL AVE

ECHO PARK AVE

DONALDSON ST

START
FINISH

BAXTER ST

PRESTON AVE

FARGO ST

ELYSIAN HEIGHTS
ELEMENTARY
SCHOOL

N

FELLOWSHIP PARK
DURATION: **45 minutes**
DISTANCE: **1.5 miles**
STEPS: **148**
DIFFICULTY: **3**
BUS: **#2, 4 to Sunset/Echo Park Ave.; Pico Union/Echo Park Dash Bus**

This is a short, sweet canyon walk highlighted by a tour of Fellowship Park—but it comes with a warning: In recent years, residents have tried to close this public passage to the public, and have installed gates and locks. Most of the time these are open. If they're not, you may have to retrace your steps a bit, but you'll be retracing along some of the city's loveliest public pathways.

Begin your walk on Echo Park Avenue near the corner of Baxter Street, perhaps with a coffee or gelato at Fix, located at that intersection. Thus sated, walk one block south, to the corner of Fargo Street, and turn right.

The road turns steep right away. Trudge up, appreciating the old frame houses as you go, and head for the welcome shade at the end of the block. Once there, grab your first staircase up—a flight of 29 stairs, with a railing but no lights, installed in 1925 by C.O. Sparks. Turn right, onto Preston Avenue, and walk about 100 feet to the end of the street. Take the second staircase down 39 steps, with a railing again but no lights, to land on Baxter.

Turn left, and head uphill.

Behind you is a good view of the monstrous Baxter Street steps, featured in Walk #15. Those are for another day. For now, turn right at the corner onto Vestal Avenue, and pass under the shade of some very old oak, walnut, and olive trees. Follow Vestal, past Champlain Terrace, to the T-intersection where Donaldson Street appears on your right. On your left, find a staircase with double handrails. Take this up a quick 25 steps and onto the sloping rise of a paved pathway that runs about 100 yards, through some large cactus and past a small fruit orchard, to land on Lemoyne Street.

Turn right, and head uphill. Just ahead you will see a large concrete structure. This is the water storage reservoir that serves the Echo Park hilltop residents. It marks the edge of Fellowship Park Way, too.

This is a huge chunk of hilltop land founded by a religious group in the 1900s. A few of their residences remain, but otherwise the land has been left untouched for over half a century. So, this is precious; walk with care.

Directly ahead, across Cerro Gordo Street, you will see a set of stairs. Climb 30 steps, equipped with a rail but no lights, and then begin your descent into the wonderland of Fellowship Park. About 50 feet of paved walkway is ahead. On the left is a burbling brook, installed by one of the residents. On the right is a fine old Craftsman house, lovingly preserved. Further on are a rope swing, other homes, a hammock, and some outdoor furniture. This is actually an extension of Lemoyne St. This is a true walk-street—you might have noticed a set of five garages on Cerro Gordo, to the left of the staircase. Those belong to these houses, which otherwise have no way in or out.

The stairs and walkways continue for another 44 steps, and another 50 feet of walkway. You'll pass through a latched swing gate; please re-latch it. Then you'll come to an intersection with a trio of mailboxes on your left.

Turn left here, and walk down the unpaved pathway, into an enchanting stretch of woodland, heavy with pine, oak, walnut, Chinese elm, and palm trees. Through the trees, you will catch glimpses of Forest Lawn Memorial Park, downtown Glendale, and the San Gabriel Mountains. You may also be able to identify the cul-de-sac end of the paved road section of Fellowship Parkway, which comes up from Landa Street.

Walk on, walk on, several hundred yards as the path winds down and around. Up and to the left you will see another very old Craftsman home, built in 1902, lined with a crumbling freestone wall. On the right are other homes, hidden in the low-hanging oaks.

At the bottom of the hill, the path takes a sharp turn to the right and drops down a final 11 steps to land just across from 2235 Lake Shore Avenue.

Now, here is the warning: This gate may be locked. If it is, turn around and retrace your steps. Pick up this walk again at the bottom of the Cerro Gordo stairs, next to the water tower, heading downhill on Cerro Gordo St.

If the gate is open, go through it, step down, turn left, and walk up Lake Shore. On the right, at the signpost for Oak Glen Place, you may see a set of stairs going down. Pass these by for now (they are part of Walk #16) and continue uphill to the corner of Cerro Gordo St. instead, just past the big Spanish multiplex on the left. Turn left, admiring the many examples of old frame bungalows. At the crest of the hill, you'll come to the Cerro Gordo stairs and the water reservoir again, on your left. Continue straight ahead as Cerro Gordo bends to the right and heads downhill. A block along, across from the architectural monstrosity to the left, you'll find an open field with great views of the Downtown skyline.

Cerro Gordo gets steeper and steeper—but not steep enough to compete with a few other streets for the honor of being the steepest residential streets in the U.S. (One of the top honors apparently belongs to a section of Fargo Street, in Silver Lake, where it falls from Apex Street to Rockford Road.) Follow Cerro Gordo past Vestal and down to Echo Park Ave., and turn right. Head downhill. On the left, at the corner of Donaldson

Street, you'll see the Dash bus turnaround. Hidden beneath a spreading pepper tree, too, is a set of stairs belonging to Walk #15. Dead ahead, you'll come to the corner of Baxter, and your starting point.

PART THREE

SILVER LAKE

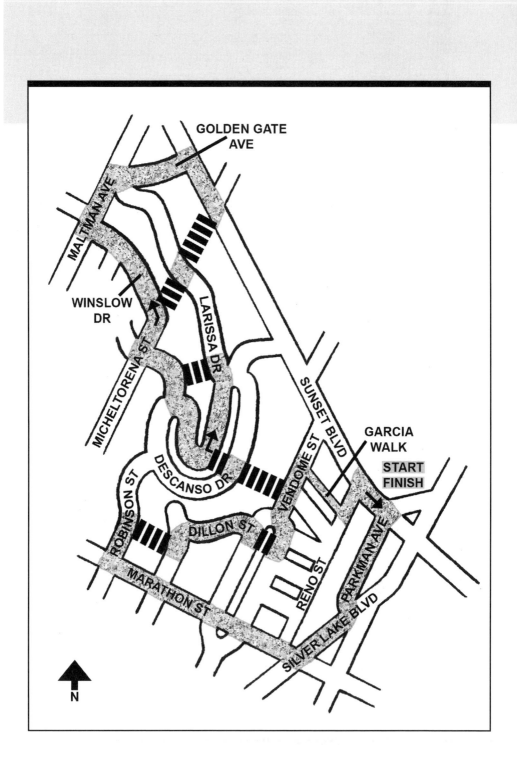

WALK #18

MUSIC BOX LOOP
DURATION: **55 minutes**
DISTANCE: **2.5 miles**
STEPS: **705**
DIFFICULTY: **3**
BUS: **#2, 4, 302, 704**

*This is a vigorous walk built around the only officially desig-
nated stairs in Silver Lake, the famous location where Laurel
and Hardy made their 1932 Academy Award-winning short*
The Music Box *for producer Hal Roach. The two comedians
had to carry a piano up the steep flight of steps between Vendome Street and Descanso Drive. All you have to do is walk
it—once up, once down—and conquer the surrounding hills.*

Begin your walk with a café con leche at Café Tropical, at the
corner of Sunset Boulevard and Parkman Avenue. Heading south
down Parkman, you may appreciate the Cold War reminder of-
fered by one of the city's few remaining air raid sirens across
the street. Enjoy, too, the peculiar Moorish apartment building
at 933 Parkman, from whose minarets the *muezzin* will never
call. At the corner of Silver Lake Boulevard, turn right. (To your
left, you can see the attractive bridge where Sunset passes over
Silver Lake. It does so because both boulevards once featured
electric streetcar lines, and it was easier to run one street under
the other than to make them into intersections. Glendale Boulevard ducks under Sunset, in Echo Park, for the same reason.)
Just before the corner, you might note the private dwelling that

used to be a church at 800 Silver Lake. At the corner itself, turn right onto Marathon Street.

Walk past the nice Florida palms, past Vendome Street and Dillon Street, and turn right onto Robinson Street. Just after the house at 830—careful, because it's easy to miss—watch for the first staircase on your right. It's a clean, well-maintained set of stairs, with a handrail and a pair of overhead streetlamps, that falls 66 steps through a pair of backyard gardens (one with an impressive collection of garden *tchotchkes*) and lands at 837 Dillon. Turn left, and walk up and around the corner.

At the end of Dillon, use the crosswalk to get to the median strip separating the two halves of Vendome, and take the 13 steps to the downhill side. Turn left. Enjoy the odd triangular park to your right and, at the stop sign, cross Vendome again to face the *Music Box* steps.

In that 1932 classic short film, Stan Laurel and Oliver Hardy were obliged to deliver a piano to the top of a steep, barren hillside, up a series of concrete stairs. Today, the hillside is covered with apartment buildings, but the stairs remain—133 steps across multiple landings, with a handrail and some overhead lights, often littered with debris, and very ill maintained for such a landmark.

At the top, you land on Descanso Drive. Continue directly across the street and take the eight rickety wooden steps to the other side of Descanso. Admiring the giant carobs (street-wrecking trees whose roots have turned the asphalt into a rippled, undulating wave), turn right and walk downhill. Along the way, you'll get nice vistas across Sunset, with good views of the steps from Hamilton Way to Elevado Street and the locked public staircase that used to carry pedestrians from Parkman Ave. to Westerly Terrace.

At the bottom of the hill, where Descanso meets Larissa Drive, catch the next staircase, going up on your left. This is a shaded, slightly crumbling staircase with a stencil at the bottom that commands, "Give Me Love." Climb the 139 steps, with a handrail and overhead lighting and a resting bench half way up, until you land on Descanso once more. Turn right, and head uphill.

At the corner, pause to admire the wild tile and sundial display on the far side of the intersection, and the more subtle tile fountain just to your right. Then turn right onto Micheltorena Street. Walk one block.

There, at the street's elbow, if you're tired or running out of time, you can cut this walk short. Go straight ahead and drop all the way down the majestic Micheltorena steps until you land on Sunset. Turn right, and walk back to Parkman. But if you are not tired or running late, turn left, onto Winslow Drive, and continue walking.

This is a charming street filled with eccentricities. Admire the asbestos-sided Craftsman at 3418 and, next door, its sign-festooned Craftsman sister. (You could spend half an hour here reading the signs warning against flooding or advertising rat poison.) Straight ahead on, at the corner of Maltman Avenue, turn right and begin your descent. After one block, bear right, still heading downhill, onto Golden Gate Avenue, and walk one more block until you hit Sunset. Turn right and head east—unless you are hungry. In the mini-mall to your left is the terrific Cuban restaurant El Cochinito, and a few doors past that is a Baskin Robbins. Go ahead. You've earned it.

Heading east on Sunset, just past the next traffic light at the corner of Sunset and Micheltorena, you will find the magnificent staircase whose top you saw a few minutes before. Now you must climb it. Enjoy the unexpected grapevines to the left and the bougainvillea overhead, and give thanks to contractor George Nichols, who built this staircase in 1925, as you go up 109 stairs to land on Larissa. Continue across Larissa as you go up the 96 stairs that return you to the top of the hill. Here again, you get a handrail and some overhead lights. (But you might want to think twice about walking here after dark. The scattered detritus suggests unwholesome nighttime activity.) Go straight on, turning left at Descanso, and beginning to retrace your steps downhill.

You'll get good views of Downtown Los Angeles on a clear day, with City Hall visible to the far left horizon. Stay on the left side of the road. Just after the house at 3279, take the wooden steps back across the divided road, then find the top of the *Music Box* staircase and climb down the 133 steps to land back on Vendome.

There's one more curiosity waiting. Cross the street, and head left. Half a block on, just past 946 Vendome, step into Garcia Walk. This is a delightful, narrow walk-street, running right through the front yards of a string of small bungalow houses. It's like the walk-streets of Venice, but with a decidedly Latino air. Admire the fine citrus, avocado, and fig trees, the roses, and the *norteño* ballads. You'll emerge at the other end onto an alley known as Reno Street. Take this to the left one block, to Sunset. Turn right and go a block to return to Parkman and Café Tropical.

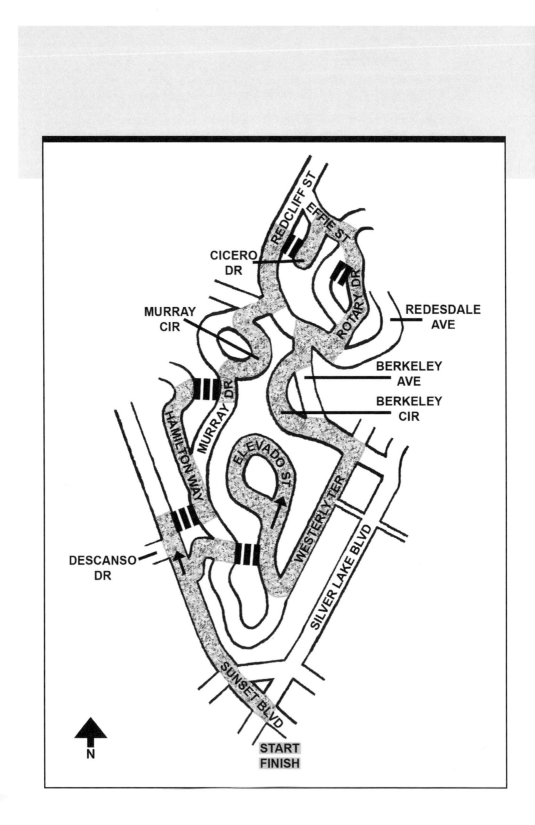

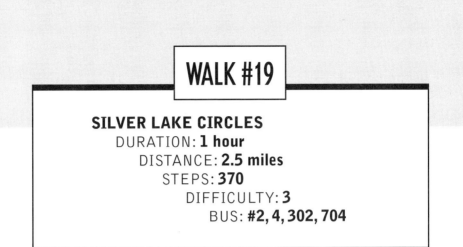

WALK #19

SILVER LAKE CIRCLES
DURATION: **1 hour**
DISTANCE: **2.5 miles**
STEPS: **370**
DIFFICULTY: **3**
BUS: **#2, 4, 302, 704**

This is a short, sweet stroll around one of Silver Lake's quietest neighborhoods, featuring shaded staircases, fine Downtown views, and a glimpse of a former Raymond Chandler home.

Begin your walk west of Sunset Boulevard and Silver Lake Boulevard, perhaps with an omelette or quiche from Dusty's Bistro, or a $1.29 taco at El Siete Mares. On the north side of Sunset, past Descanso Drive and the storefront at 3229, you'll find your first staircase going up on the right.

This is a steep set of 90 steps, without handrails or lights, which drops you at 3300 Hamilton Way. Turn left, heading slightly downhill. Just after 3359, take the second set of stairs, also on the right—this one with a handrail, but no lights—climbing 83 steps to drop you at 1513 Murray Drive. Go left and up, briefly, then turn right onto Murray Circle.

This is one of Silver Lake's most charming hidden neighborhoods, so bucolic and quiet that people have lawn chairs in their *front* yards. At the end of the short circle, pay particular attention to the fantastic cactus forest spreading across the yards at 1568 and 1570.

Just after that, turn right, back onto Murray Dr., and

head downhill. Where Murray meets Berkeley Avenue, turn left and up. As you pass the garage at 1630, turn right onto the next set of stairs, appreciating the handrail and, overhead, a night-light supplied by one of the local residents. Climb the 90 steps to 1677 Cicero Drive, and turn left. Like Murray, this is a quiet corner of Silver Lake with some good old wooden houses and, at 1650, some handsome tile work. Up and to the left, as you approach the corner, you can also catch glimpses of the Paramour Mansion, the current incarnation of the old Canfield-Moreno Estate at the top of the Micheltorena hill. Once a stately private residence, later a Catholic home for wayward women, and then a nunnery, it is now a busy film location and party venue.

At Effie Street, turn right. Go up and over the small rise and, as you cross Dillon, take advantage of Silver Lake's shortest staircase—a little five-step number at the southeast corner. Continue straight ahead, onto Rotary, down and around the side of the hill, enjoying some good views of Downtown and, high up to the left, the identical cookie-cutter houses of the Hathaway Hills Estates, Silver Lake's only gated community.

At the corner of Rotary and Redesdale Avenue, turn left and walk a short distance to 1639. Here, in this duplex, Los Angeles's premiere detective writer Raymond Chandler is said to have hung his hat for a spell. When you've enjoyed that, retrace your steps past Effie, down to Berkeley Ave., and turn left. Then turn right immediately onto Berkeley Circle.

Like Murray and Cicero, this is a quiet block with some interesting architectural features—a couple of good-looking Spanish adobes and modern wood-and-steel blockades. Check out the ruby-red slipper sculpture at 3100.

Bear right, back onto Berkeley, and then turn right onto Westerly Terrace. Head uphill, enjoying the shade from the Chinese elms and carobs. Note the pedestrian pathway coming in on your left, just after 1458. This is the western terminus of Scott Avenue, which runs through start-and-stop sections all the way to Elysian Park and Dodger Stadium. Carry on up, then turn right onto Elevado St.

As with Murray, this is a suburban circle street, quiet and calm. Note the subtle shaded charms of 1500, the marvelous Indian palace with the elephant frescoes at 1515—a house owned at one point by actress Lily Tomlin—and the pair of handsome wooden Craftsman homes at 1622 and 1626.

Turn right as you complete the circle, and walk just past the house at 1435, and take the final staircase going down on the right. This is an elegant set of 102 steps, running past a little truck garden on the left and some interesting tile work on the right.

You land on Westerly. Up and to the left, on the right-hand side of the road, is a beautiful set of stairs dropping down to Parkman Ave. But you can't use it. The staircase has been locked against the public since the 1980s, when it was the playground of drug dealers and users. Instead, turn right down Westerly, and then turn left onto Sunset and return to your starting point.

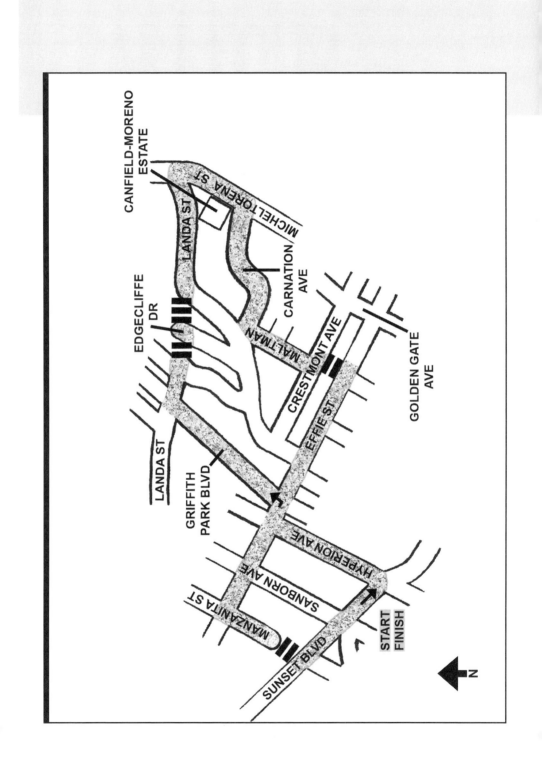

SUNSET JUNCTION LOOP
DURATION: **45 minutes**
DISTANCE: **2 miles**
STEPS: **305**
DIFFICULTY: **3.5**
BUS: **#2, 4, 302, 704**

This is a short walk with steep steps, steep hills, and huge views from the mountains to the sea. It's a great workout, concluding with a rewarding plethora of coffee and dessert destinations.

Begin your walk at Sunset Junction, the historic crossing of Sunset and Santa Monica Boulevard with Sanborn Avenue. Walk east a block to Hyperion Avenue, take a left, and head for the hills.

The walk starts dully, broken up by views of the Franklin Hills and Griffith Observatory, off to the left. When you get to Effie Street, turn right, then left again at once onto Griffith Park Boulevard. Walk one long block and turn right onto Landa Street.

The ascent begins. Take the slope or the 19 sidewalk-stairs on the left. At Lucile Avenue, cross the intersection and find your first staircase.

This one has a rail on one side, but no lights, and runs a straight 92 steps without a break. You land at 3701 Landa, where this walk-street meets the cul-de-sac end of Edgecliffe Drive. Cross the intersection, and continue onto the next staircase.

This one also has a rail, and is without lights, and runs a long 154 steps over several landings and walkways. It's a true walk-street, too: the houses on the right have no other access. They are served by garages on the block above, but the staircase is the only way in and out. Pity the piano movers and big appliance deliverers.

New bungalows with addresses on Lucile below have been built on the left. Above them are good views of the Franklin Hills and beyond, up the Hyperion gulch into Glendale. Continue up the last of the steps, and land at the corner where Landa becomes Maltman Avenue. Continue your ascent, up and to the left.

The enormous retaining wall, topped with old wrought iron fencing, is the outer perimeter of the historic Canfield-Moreno Estate. This 22,000-square-foot Spanish Revival villa, originally known as Crestmount, was built by silent film star Antonio Moreno and his oil heiress wife Daisy Canfield Danziger. (He appeared opposite Dorothy Gish, Gloria Swanson, and Pola Negri. She died in an automobile accident 10 years after the construction of the estate.) The home was designed by Robert D. Farquhar, who also designed Beverly Hills High School, the lovely California Club building in Downtown Los Angeles, and the stately William Andrews Clark Memorial Library near USC.

As you climb Landa, you will see increasing evidence of the vast estate. Asian-influenced gates appear on the right, and outlines of outbuildings behind them. As you reach Micheltorena Street and turn right, continuing up the hill and around the parameter of the estate, you may begin to understand the appeal of the location. Behind you are views of Glendale and Burbank, and off to your left are views of the San Gabriel Mountains. Ahead, as you meet the crest, you can see the skyscrapers of Downtown and the historic buildings of the Wilshire Corridor straight ahead. Further down, you will see the western views as well.

For now, you find yourself at the gates of the Paramour Mansion, as the estate is now known. Following Canfield's death, the estate became a school for wayward girls, and later a convent for Franciscan nuns. The Silver Lake restaurant entrepreneur Dana Hollister took charge of the place in 1998, and has since leased or loaned it to musicians, filmmakers, and philanthropists, who have used the location for fundraisers, music videos, reality TV shows, movies, and lavish parties. Lucinda Williams, Sarah McLachlan, Gwen Stefani, Fiona Apple, and Little Big Band guitar sensation Colin James have all recorded albums there. The Red Hot Chili Peppers, Sting, and Elton John have all performed there.

Past the Paramour gates—which still bear the "C" and "M" initials of the estate's original tenants—the road slopes down sharply. (How sharply? So sharply that it was once used for hill climbs. A *Los Angeles Times* story from 1932 boasted that the new Essex Terraplane automobile had crested the Micheltorena summit at a record-breaking 39 mph.) Follow Micheltorena and take the first right, onto Carnation Avenue. As this alley-like street opens up, you'll get fine views from East Hollywood to West Hollywood, to Century City and Westwood and, on very clear days, the Pacific Ocean. Follow Carnation to the first corner, and turn left onto Maltman Ave. Drop down a block to Crestmont Avenue, then catch the pedestrian-only block of Maltman that falls to Effie St.—a wide garden of cacti, flanked by sidewalks that might have been a paved street at some point. At Effie, look across the intersection at the fine Craftsman residence at 1664. This is the August House, a 1913 structure that is one of Silver Lake's oldest residences.

For a little more local color, you may turn left onto Effie, go a block to Golden Gate Avenue, and walk a block downhill to 1614. This historic bungalow was once the home of silent cowboy star (and early Silver Lake resident) Tom Mix, who lived here in 1918 and later bought substantial holdings around Glendale Boulevard.

Otherwise, turn right onto Effie and head west. Follow Effie along as it rises and falls down toward Griffith Park Boulevard. Enjoy the views of East Hollywood. Many of the big buildings directly in front of you are parts of Kaiser Permanente

Hospital. The big blue buildings are parts of the Church of Scientology.

Cross Griffith Park Blvd., Hyperion, and Sanborn Avenue. Continue to Manzanita Street, and turn left. After a block of small, fragrant fruit orchards and a few good examples of Florida palms, find your last staircase—a set of 40 steps, with handrails and overhead lights, bisecting the charming Manzanita Street Community Garden. At the top, where the steps meet Sunset, turn left. Walk a block to Sanborn, and back to your starting poin

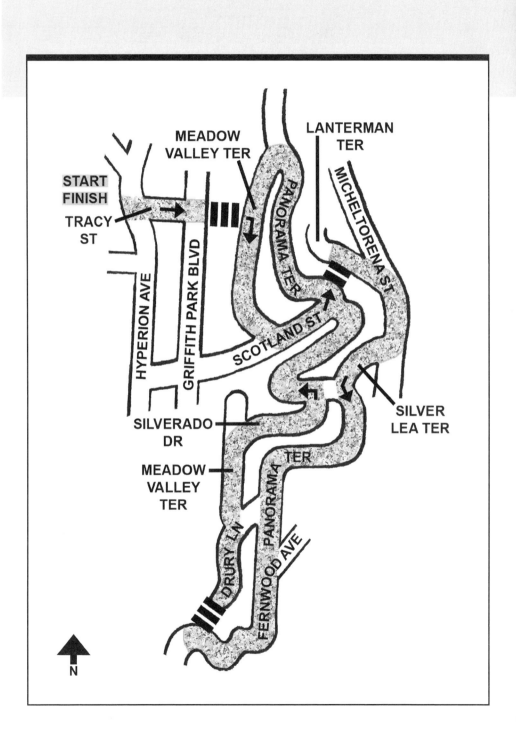

SILVER LAKE TERRACES WEST
DURATION: **1 hour**
DISTANCE: **2.5 miles**
STEPS: **190**
DIFFICULTY: **2.5**
BUS: **#175**

This is a fairly easy walk on the western-facing slopes of Silver Lake's Hyperion gulch, crisscrossing a series of "terrace" streets dotted with architectural delights. It doesn't have a lot of steps, but it's a bracing short stroll.

Begin your walk at the corner of Hyperion Avenue and Tracy Street, perhaps after a slice from the fine local pizzeria Tomato Pie, or a bit of home improvement guidance from Baller Hardware, Silver Lake's treasured hardware store. Either way, leave Hyperion, with the pizza and the plumber's tape behind you, and walk east on Tracy.

The big ship-shaped building on the right is The Boat, a recording studio (Beck recorded most of the 2005 album *Guero* here) that used to be known as "The Good Ship Grace" and was home to the Haven of Rest radio ministry. (The Haven, without the ship, later moved down to 2410 Hyperion.) Across the street is another of those old air raid sirens, a sad relic of 1950s Cold War paranoia.

Continue down Tracy and across Griffith Park Boulevard to your first staircase. It starts as a sloping walkway dead ahead, between 2424 and 2428 Griffith Park, passing a piece of open ground with fruit trees on it, then up 23 steps to land at 2425 Meadow Valley Terrace. Turn right.

Meadow Valley Terrace, despite its rather redundant name, is a nice flat street running parallel to Griffith Park. It hasn't much to recommend it, except its welcome quiet, a couple of stands of Florida palms and a good-looking Indonesian teak gate at 2335.

Continue a bit to the corner of Scotland Street, and turn left. Rise up past the exceptional redwood tree in front of 3022. At the next corner, where Scotland meets Panorama Terrace, bear left again and find your next staircase. It begins on the right, just after the house at 2366, and includes eight steps, a long walkway, and a steep 43 steps to the top.

This is another terrace—Lanterman Terrace. Turn right, and head up the little stretch of steep street. At the corner, bear right onto Micheltorena Street, noticing the simple green-hued house at 2323 as you pass. This is the Tierman House, a 1940 Gregory Ain home that was named a Historic-Cultural Monument No. 124 for its elegant simplicity. (There are many other Ain houses in the area, including one at 2404 Micheltorena and the amazing Avenal Cooperative Housing Project, near The Coffee Table on Rowena Avenue.)

Press on, and then turn right down Silver Lea Terrace. There are ocean views here on a clear day, and views of Griffith Park, the Observatory, and the Hollywood sign on most other days. The houses are a mix of Spanish-style adobe and midcentury modern. Walk a few minutes, and then bear left where Silver Lea meets Panorama Terrace. Enjoy the flat walk, pausing to appreciate the "Surfers Rule" concrete carving in the street just after 2237. Continue straight on as Panorama passes Drury Lane—amusing yourself with *Shrek* and Muffin Man references— and continues uphill. At the top, bear right as Panorama turns into Fernwood Avenue. Head downhill.

Up and to your left you'll see a group of late-fifties, arch-roof homes designed by Alan Siskind. Further on, at 3228 Fernwood, there's an interesting boxy hillside home designed more recently by Malibu architect Lorcan O'Herlihy.

Follow Fernwood down and around. Past the house at 3315, on the right, look for your next staircase. This is a steep, L-shaped set of stairs, consisting of 93 steps. It used to be covered by a beautiful stand of eucalyptus trees, which were cut down by some shade-hating barbarian.

You land at 2009 Drury. Walk uphill from the cul-de-sac, appreciating the fine flowering ginger on the left and the groups of Florida palms on the right. Coming down the other side, bear left back onto Meadow Valley Terrace, admiring the tiny turreted tower on the house at 3217. At the bottom of the hill, turn right onto Silverado Drive.

(It would appear that you could continue straight on Meadow Valley Terrace, back to the section you walked earlier, but for some reason lost to history, the road stops abruptly just ahead, then starts again a half-block later. Squat in the middle of the two ends of the street sits one single-family residence, through which you cannot pass.)

Instead, go up Silverado, walking beneath a horticultural amusement park that includes oak, bamboo, magnolia, and more, to where it meets Panorama. Turn left and stroll along, welcoming the flat and downhill sections, and not failing to appreciate the Bob's Big Boy statuette on the porch at 2354. At the intersection with Scotland, bear right, past the staircase you climbed earlier, and continue on Panorama. Rounding the corner, note the charming English "inn" at 2387. But don't be tempted by the many private staircases rising on the right.

At the next corner, on your left, do not miss the unusual Spanish house at 2459. It has stained glass windows and an extravagance of tiled scenes on the adobe walls, featuring portraits of life in Taxco, Mexico. Turn the corner, bearing left, and drop downhill, back onto Meadow Valley Terrace. Just after 2431, you'll find the first staircase again on your right. Head down the steps and the walkway, cross Griffith Park, continue to Hyperion, and you will have completed the hike.

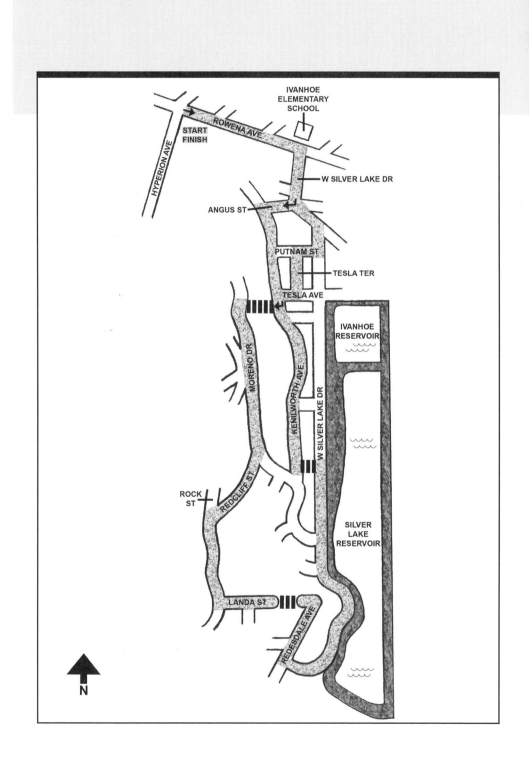

COFFEE TABLE LOOP
DURATION: **1 hour, 15 minutes**
DISTANCE: **3.5 miles**
STEPS: **268**
DIFFICULTY: **3**
BUS: **#175, 201**

This is a gentle, flat walk interrupted by hidden staircases and towering views of Downtown Los Angeles and the San Gabriel Mountains, as well as up-close snapshots of the Silver Lake Reservoir and some of the community's most treasured architectural gems.

Commence walking at or near The Coffee Table, a genial café at 2930 Rowena Avenue, just east of the corner of Rowena and Hyperion Avenue. Begin walking east on Rowena, toward Ivanhoe Elementary School on your left and Camelot Kids Pre-school on your right. Turn right at West Silver Lake Drive and head south.

At the second corner, turn right onto Angus Street. After a quick block and a short uphill, turn left onto Kenilworth Avenue. This walk is a botanical garden of big Silver Lake trees, and they start here. Kenilworth is lined with magnificent examples of eucalyptus trees, particularly the tall, elephant-legged lemon eucalyptus. Further on, as you approach the corner of Putnam Street, you will find equally fine examples of the flowering purple jacaranda. Stroll along, admiring homes designed in the Spanish style, many of them adorned with wooden-railed balconies and porches.

At the corner of Tesla Avenue, just after the house at 2421, find your first staircase on the right. This is a 1926 construction from McCray Co., rising 111 steps over four flights and a long sloping walkway. It has no rails and no street lights, but it does afford fine views of the Silver Lake Reservoir and hills beyond.

The reservoir and community are named not for the color, but for Herman Silver, a Los Angeles Board of Water commissioner who helped design the lake. Local legend says that three of them—Myra, Effie, and Lucile—are named after Silver's three daughters.

Land at the top at 2358 Moreno Drive, and turn left. Be warned: You are now in Walking Doctor territory. The famously bronzed Silver Lake stroller—a general practitioner and long-time Silver Lake resident—can be seen marching furiously forward through the area day and night, in fair weather and foul. (He's the subject of a documentary short film called *Walking Man*.) Smile and walk on.

You are now on the flats again. Bear left at the intersection with Micheltorena Street, gradually sloping down, slowing to admire the odd Mickey Mouse water feature at 2277. Old city maps show a public staircase here, dropping from Moreno to Kenilworth to West Silver Lake Dr. There *ought* to be one, but there isn't. So, instead, continue down Moreno to the corner of Redcliff Street.

For a diversion, continue down Moreno to the next corner, which is Kenilworth, and turn right. There, at number 2178, is the old "hunting lodge" home of entrepreneur and philanthropist George C. Page—the same one who funded the museum by the La Brea Tar Pits. His 1937 Silver Lake mansion had its front door up the hill on Moreno, and its hunting lodge section down below. The lower section is all that remains of the once-grand estate. It still features fine heavy timbers and leaded glass windows.

Back at the corner of Moreno and Redcliff, head uphill

for a much more compelling architectural wonder. Just up to your right you will see the cantilevered tennis court belonging to Silvertop, the remarkable 1957 wonder from architect John Lautner. You can't see the house from here, but you will be able to later.

Next door to Silvertop, as you climb Redcliff, you may pause to admire the hidden interior elevator at 2129. This is one of only three in Silver Lake, and is designed to take some of the climb out of getting from the street up to the hillside home. Press on, bearing left at the corner of Redcliff and Rock Street. On the left you'll stroll under some attractive silk floss trees. On the right, you'll pass the 1937 C.J. Berne residence, designed by C. Raimond Johnson, who also designed UCLA's Kerckhoff Hall.

At the corner, turn left on Landa Street, taking in good Downtown views as you drop down and catching your breath as you climb up. At the crest, dig the charming and charmingly named El Do Bo Bi house on the right. No idea what that means, but the Spanish style home stands at the brink of the grand East Landa stairs. Stop here and gaze.

From the top are marvelous views of the reservoir and the San Gabriel Mountains beyond—snow-capped in winter. From the first landing down are views of the grand Garbutt-Hathaway Estate, on the hill rising highest to your right. This is an all-concrete construction—even the "wood" beam interior is poured concrete—built in 1926 for Frank Garbutt, an inventor and movie pioneer who suffered from a terror of house fires. From the second landing, you can see Glendale and Forest Lawn Memorial Park, the setting for Evelyn Waugh's satiric novel *The Loved One* and the final resting place of Humphrey Bogart, Mary Pickford, and dozens of other big-name Hollywood stars. From the third, here is the fine Silver Lake "meadow," a piece of reservoir-adjacent land recently opened to the public. From the fourth, straight ahead, lie the concealed Fargo Street steps, a substantial Silver Lake public staircase locked and closed to the public.

It's 84 steps in all, dropping you at 2026 Landa. Walk to

the corner, and turn right onto Redesdale Avenue. A bit on, slow to appreciate the blue-tiled Asian architecture at 1954, the residence of designer David Hyun, who was also responsible for the Japanese Village Plaza in Little Tokyo, and is the son of one of the founders of the Republic of Korea. Pass by, continuing down to the bottom of Redesdale, then cross carefully to the east side of West Silver Lake Dr. and begin your stroll along the reservoir.

The city has recently planted redwoods here and prepared a fine decomposed granite walkway. Wind along and around, taking your place among the joggers and dog-walkers. On the way, you will get good looks at the beautiful Cove steps, across the lake (featured in Walk #26) and the fine arched lines of Lautner's Silvertop, high up to the right. Also on the right, going along, you may get glimpses of nesting egrets. These elegant, long-legged birds take up residence in the eucalyptus trees that line the lake. They nest in winter and produce fledglings in spring, and are marvelous to behold in flight.

Cross the busy boulevard, carefully again, and find the next set of stairs just after the house at 2171. This is another Mc-Cray Co. construction from 1926, rising 73 stairs over several flights and another sloping walkway, and again without handrails or lights. At the top, turn right onto Kenilworth and begin the walk home. Here are more fine lemon eucalyptus, and Spanish-style homes with delightful porches and porticoes. On the front of one home you may see a stenciled letter V and, under it, the Morse code for that letter. That's a dot-dot-dot-dash, which also describes the opening notes of Beethoven's Fifth, and the Roman numeral for five is "V"—you think about such things, when you stairwalk.

Turn right on Tesla Avenue—or take the stairs up and do another loop—and walk a short block down to Tesla Terrace, and turn left. Here again are nice Spanish haciendas with nice hanging balconies. At the corner, turn right onto Putnam, under the cover of weeping willows and those purple jacarandas, and then turn left onto West Silver Lake. Jog back around to Rowena, and turn left, and find yourself back at the beginning of your walk.

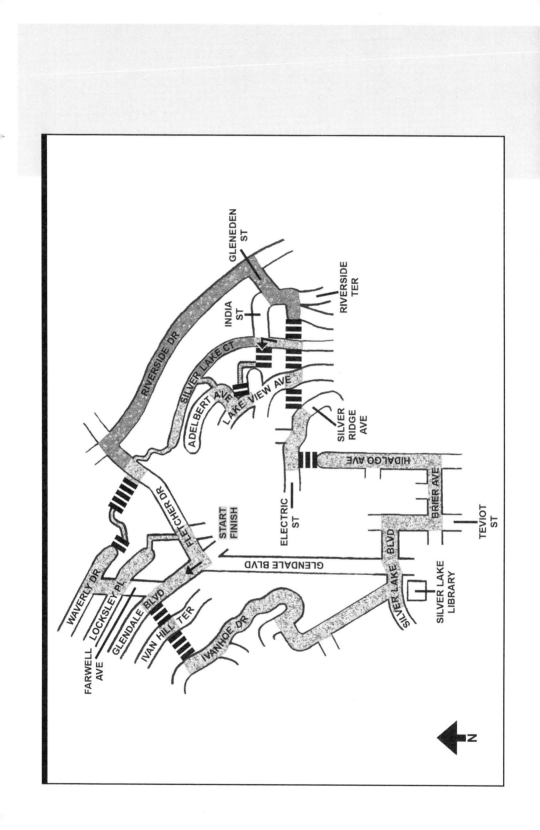

WALK #23

ASTRO LOOP
DURATION: **1 hour, 30 minutes**
DISTANCE: **3 miles**
STEPS: **674**
DIFFICULTY: **4.5**
BUS: **#92, 603**

This is a rugged walk, requiring strong legs and good shoes, and not recommended on wet days . . . but what a walk! It features Silver Lake views, super-secret stairways, and a stroll along unpaved roads that used to be Red Car trolley lines.

Begin your walk with a coffee at the Starbucks at the corner of Glendale Boulevard and Fletcher Drive, or a meal at the Googie-style Astro Family Restaurant—a 1950s futuristic diner designed by Louis Armet and Eldon Davis, the architects responsible for the look of the beloved and historic Ship's and Norm's coffee shops that once graced the city. (There still is one classic Norm's in business, on La Cienega Boulevard near Rosewood Avenue. A classic Norm's sign, without the Googie building, still stands over a more modern Norm's near Pico Boulevard and Sepulveda Boulevard.) Start out heading west on Glendale, using the complicated network of crosswalks to get on the south side of the street. Just after the house at 2617 Glendale, find the first staircase going up.

It's well hidden, and usually well maintained, rising 56 steps to where it crosses Ivan Hill Terrace and another 156 to where it meets Ivanhoe Drive. (Both are Bert Pollock constructions from 1925.) At the top, catch your breath and admire the peculiar castle at 2605. Judy Garland lived here with her mother and sister in 1933, when she was still known as Frances Gumm. Fifty years later or so, Eric Roberts took up residence. Over the fence, if you sneak a peek, you can see a variety of terraces and pools. It must once have been grand.

Turn left and head up the hill, staying on Ivanhoe as it bears right and then winds up, down, and around. Don't take the right turns onto Lindsay Lane or Edgewater Terrace. Instead, go straight on to Silver Lake Boulevard, then turn left, go to the corner, cross Silver Lake and then cross Glendale Blvd. in front of the new public library building. Once over, continue on Silver Lake Blvd., turning right at the corner of Teviot Street and left onto Brier Avenue. Go two blocks up the hill—glancing back to get a nice view of the reservoir and of architect John Lautner's famous Silvertop house on the hill behind—and turn left onto Hidalgo Avenue. Follow Hidalgo, down the slope and back up, to the cul-de-sac ending.

Here is your next staircase, a delightful wide set of stairs, 82 in all, bordered by a fine fruit orchard. Turn right at the bottom, onto Electric Street. Then walk straight up the hill, as Electric veers into Silver Ridge Avenue, past a fine example of modern Silver Lake architecture from local Barbara Bestor on the right. Half a block on, on the left, watch for a very discreet staircase that comes in just at 2494.

This is a shady bower, 77 steps down onto Lake View Avenue, and another 31 steps and a walkway down onto Silver Lake Court.

There are even some Silver Lake locals who haven't heard of Silver Lake Court, a wide, unpaved stretch of dirt road that runs parallel to Riverside Drive and the noisy I-5 freeway. This piece of open land was once the route of the Red Car electric trolley line that ran from Downtown Los Angeles out to the communities of Atwater Village and Glendale. The trolley ran straight through this section of the community, then known as "Edendale."

The staircase ahead continues down to Riverside Place. Ignore that, and instead turn left onto the unpaved Silver Lake Court, and walk approximately 90 yards. There, just before India Street comes in on your right, bear left and walk through the grass up the slope. You'll see a flight of fine-looking concrete steps with short columns on either side. Don't take these—it's a private set of stairs leading into a backyard. Instead, press on up the hill, following the line of the redwood-stained fence on your left. At the end of the fence, hidden by bushes and overgrowth, you'll find the real public stairs.

Despite their hidden location, these stairs are well maintained and clean, rising 98 steps across many flights, with a latched swing gate in the middle. At the top of the hill, turn right at once onto the driveway ahead of you. When the driveway turns to sidewalk, turn left and take the staircase going down— 35 steps down onto Lake View Avenue.

Turn right. Walk half a block, and then turn right again onto Adelbert Avenue. Cruise down and around and, just past the house at 2620, step onto the path on your right and walk down the short slope and back onto Silver Lake Court. Go left.

You will shortly find yourself at the edge of a hill high above the intersection of Fletcher and Riverside Drives. In the near distance is the green swath of Forest Lawn, Glendale's famous memorial park and cemetery. Closer, and louder, is the roaring I-5 freeway. Directly down the hill you will see the concrete footings of the old Fletcher Red Car Viaduct.

They supported quite a structure. The viaduct carried trolley passengers over a 500-foot-long, 40-foot-high wooden trestle (built in 1906) that crossed the gulch through which Fletcher now runs. From there, the trolley tracks continued along Riverside Dr., and out to Atwater Village. (The footings for that bridge still remain, marooned midstream in the Los Angeles River.) The trolley line was decommissioned in 1955, and the viaduct was dismantled in 1959. Half a century later, in 2003, the Fletcher Red Car Trestle Footings received their official designation from the city of Los Angeles as Historic-Cultural Monument No. 770.

Make your way carefully down the slope—or, don't. If the path is too challenging—it is dangerous when it's wet, and can be slippery in very dry weather, too—double back, following the unpaved Silver Lake Court, retracing your footsteps past the turning for India St. Then take the short stairway down to your left. It drops 30 steps onto Riverside Terrace. Take a left, veer right and down, and then turn left onto Riverside Drive. Turn left and follow Riverside until it reaches Fletcher. You'll see the trestle footings up and to the left, behind the gas station.

Whichever route you've taken, use the crosswalk to get to the other side of Fletcher. Then use the parking lot for Home Restaurant to access the stairway rising up the opposite side of the Fletcher Viaduct.

This is a set of 64 steps rising straight up, decorated with local gang graffiti, which sometimes features a small hobo camp off to its left side. At the top, bear left and follow the side-walk 100 yards or so, then take the next staircase going up to the right—45 steps, over many graffiti-strewn risers stamped with a contractor's stamp reading "Tomei Construction 1934," that will land you at the cul-de-sac end of Waverly Drive. Enjoy the sweeping sycamore trees and the quiet, for one block, and then turn left onto Farwell Avenue. After one block, take a left onto Locksley Place. Follow this down to the cul-de-sac end. There, on the left-hand side, find the narrow walkway leading back to-ward the stairways you've just taken. This time, though, take the first sidewalk turning to the right, go through the swing gate, and find yourself back on Fletcher. Turn right, go to the corner, and make your way back to your starting point.

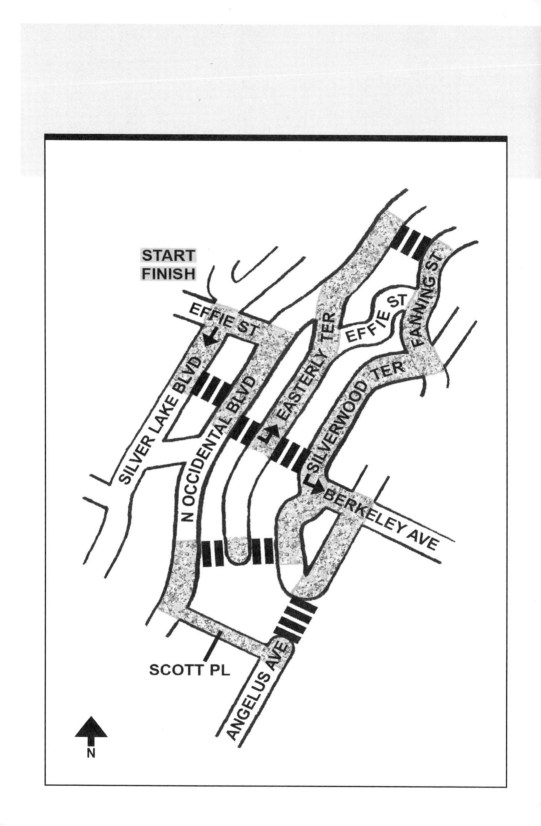

SILVER LAKE TERRACES EAST
DURATION: **45 minutes**
DISTANCE: **2 miles**
STEPS: **762**
DIFFICULTY: **3**
BUS: **#201**

The steep slopes of the Silver Lake Boulevard gulch offer dramatic staircases on both sides. This western-facing episode delivers great Moderne architecture, fine mountain and city views and a real workout.

Start walking from the corner of Silver Lake Boulevard and Effie Street, perhaps after a hand-hewn cup of coffee at LAMILL Coffee Boutique. Thus fortified, walk south on Silver Lake, just past the historic "Market Building." Duck into the walkway on your left and find the first staircase going up. This is a short flight of 25 stairs that lands you on N. Occidental Boulevard. Go right. Just after the house at 1606, find the next staircase to your left. It doesn't have a handrail, except at the top, and it's steep, and it's 76 steps. Huff and puff.

These stairs continue across the street. Don't go with them. Instead, turn left, onto Easterly Terrace, and enjoy the flat ground for a while. Walk through this gentrifying section of Silver Lake, admiring the crumbling private staircases on the right, past the turning for Effie on the right and Occidental on the left. Below you, on Silver Lake Blvd., is the trendy music venue Spaceland.

Farther on, just across from the house at 1809, find the next set of stairs. This is a massive tower of risers, 108 steps in a single, unbroken flight, without handrails. Climb up, onto Fanning Street and turn right. As you catch your breath, look across the Silver Lake Blvd. gulch to see the Swan Place steps (also seen on Walk #25) rising on the opposite hillside.

Fanning meets Effie. Bear left, and head uphill. At the next turning, if such architectural matters interest you, turn left onto Silverwood Terrace and go about four houses in. On the right, in deep blue, is another of those hillside houses with its own elevator, encased in a silo-like tower that meets the street. If such things don't interest you, bear right, turning slightly downhill, onto Silverwood.

There are good westerly views here, all the way to Century City, the Getty Center, and the Pacific Ocean on clear days. Follow the street down as it turns and flattens into a narrow terrace. At 1709 is a William Kesling-designed, Moderne-esque home from 1936. (There's another just back at 2808 Effie. You will get an opportunity to see even better examples farther along on this walk.)

Just after the house at 1617, you will see a staircase going down. Don't take it. Instead, go straight on to the turning at Berkeley Avenue. Turn left, and then right onto Angelus Avenue, and walk one long block down to the bend in the road. There you will find the next staircase.

Someone has placed a bench at the top of the stairs, handy if you're coming up. For going down, enjoy the wide staircase with no rails, but elegant in design, falling 177 steps down multiple flights and past several houses that have no other access. Pity the piano movers! At the bottom, under the shade of a huge date palm, hang a hard right and go past the gate blocking car access to the alley. This is actually part of Scott Place, a thin street that runs from western Silver Lake all the way to Dodger Stadium—with occasional interruptions, like the one you're on. Take this downhill for one block, and then turn right onto N. Occidental Blvd.

Now comes the hiking. Just opposite the house at 1483, find the next staircase to your right. This is a steep flight of 82 steps—courtesy of Given-Wolverhaupten, 1927—with a handrail, lifting you up to the cul-de-sac end of Easterly Terrace. Cross the cul-de-sac, and continue up—another steep flight, this one of 89 steps, with a handrail, through a fine little forest of deep green bamboo.

You land at 1525 Silverwood. Take a left, and stroll along the flat section of this quiet block, past the turning you took earlier for Berkeley, while looking for the stairs you passed once before at 1617 Silverwood—now on your left. Take these stairs for a long drop of 104 steps, landing you back on Easterly Terrace.

For an architectural sidestep, go left about 50 paces to the twin marvels of Skinner House and Vanderpool House. The stark white side-by-side homes, both built from 1936 to 1937, are the best extant examples of the designer William Kesling's Streamline Moderne residences. Kesling, whose office was near the starting point of this walk, at 1639 Silver Lake Blvd., was called by his biographer the "Rogue Architect of Streamline Moderne," and had been Rudolph Schindler's draftsman before striking out on his own. You can see one of his earliest examples, "Model Home," further on down the block at 1519.

That done, retrace your steps along Easterly, and take the final staircase down, just past the house at 1547. Landing on Occidental, turn right and walk toward the intersection with Effie. Turn left, walk to Silver Lake Blvd., and you are done.

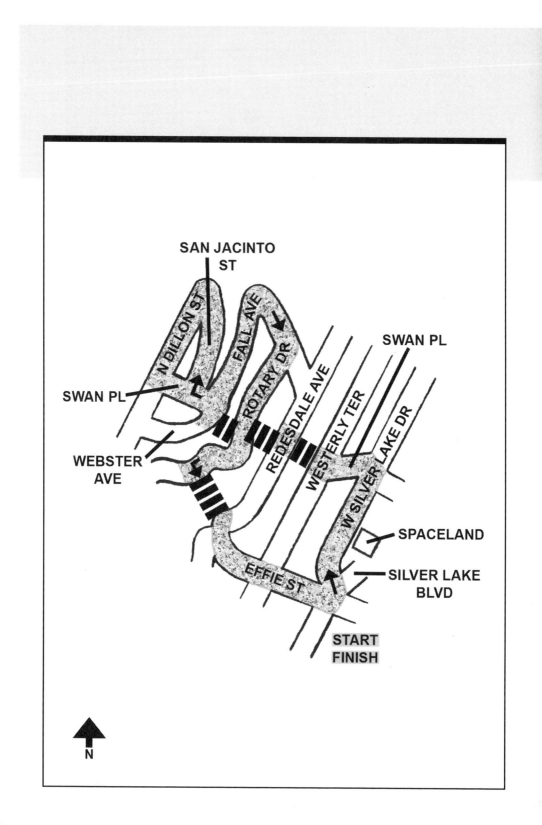

SAN JACINTO ST

N DILLON ST

FALL AVE

ROTARY DR

SWAN PL

SWAN PL

REDESDALE AVE

WESTERLY TER

W SILVER LAKE DR

WEBSTER AVE

SPACELAND

EFFIE ST

SILVER LAKE BLVD

START FINISH

N

WALK #25

SWAN'S WAY
DURATION: **40 minutes**
DISTANCE: **1.5 miles**
STEPS: **369**
DIFFICULTY: **4**
BUS: **#201**

Here's an intriguing combination—a short walk with some really steep steps. This is a Silver Lake circuit with great views, interesting houses, and some of the longest, steepest staircases in the city, great for cross-training and cardio.

Start your walk at the intersection of Effie Street and Silver Lake Boulevard, perhaps with a café latte from the LAMILL Coffee Boutique or a Slurpie from 7–Eleven. Then head north, veering slightly left, onto West Silver Lake Drive. This will take you behind Silver Lake's indie music venue, Spaceland, and lead you to Swan Place. Take a left, go a very short block to Westerly Terrace, and find the first staircase.

It's a sharp 77 steps straight up without a break, offering nice shade from the sun, but no handrails except at the bottom. At the top, you land at 1760 Redesdale Avenue. Cross the street, and grab the second set of stairs. This one features an L-shaped landing, good handrails, and a straight shot of 110 stairs to the top. It also offers some good views of the Silver Lake Reservoir and dog park, and the fantastic Garbutt House (detailed in Walk #22), the area's historic all-concrete, flameproof estate across the canyon, barricaded inside Silver Lake's only gated community, Hathaway Hill Estates.

You land at 1780 Rotary Drive. Directly across the street, you'll find the third set of stairs. Like the last one, this has an L-shaped approach and was inspected and approved by one J.H. Rothwell, and shoots straight up 100 stairs without a break.

Head uphill, into the intersection, and follow Swan Place to the left. Then turn right at the first corner, onto San Jacinto Street. There are some fine cactus gardens here, at 1809 and 1823, and an excess of Moorish sentiment at 1824—fine, arched doorways, a tiled dome and a whimsical minaret. At the corner, where San Jacinto bends to the left and turns into N. Dillon Street, you may observe the house at 1830. This is the Loeb Estate, a 1940 design by Sumner Spaulding—the architect best known for having designed the famous Avalon Casino on Catalina Island.

Continue down Dillon, slowing to admire the house at 1843. This is the Lipetz House, from designer Raphael Soriano. A student of Richard Neutra and Rudolph Schindler, and a contemporary of Gregory Ain and Harwell Hamilton Harris, Soriano built this ship-shaped house in 1936, in part as a music performance space. Inside the living area, if the curtains are open, you can see curved walls lined with banquette seating for the audience.

Continue down Dillon, and turn left onto Swan again, and then left onto Webster Avenue. Follow this downhill, where the Moorish architecture from up the hill has found an echo at "Quinta Diana," a house at 1836. Continue down where Webster turns into Fall Avenue, and then turn right onto Rotary Dr. at the next corner.

Rotary rises up, crests and passes the Swan staircases you walked earlier. Continue on, mindful of the cars—this is a narrow street, without sidewalks—to just past the house at 1724. On your left, you'll find the last staircase, a lovely, shaded, secluded set of 82 steps that drops you off at 1705 Redesdale. Walk straight ahead and down, back onto Effie. At the stoplight, you will be back at Silver Lake Blvd., and your starting point.

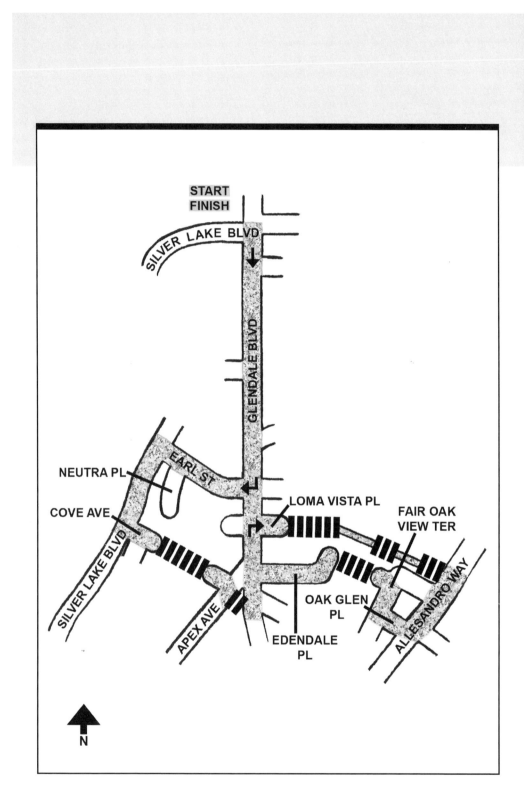

COVE-LOMA VISTA LOOP
DURATION: **1 hour**
DISTANCE: **2.2 miles**
STEPS: **664**
DIFFICULTY: **4**
BUS: **#92**

This is perhaps the most arduous and most beautiful of Silver Lake walks, up and down the sides of two hills, with towering views of the reservoir, the Hollywood Hills, the San Gabriel Mountains, and more, as well as some wild architecture and some curious local history.

Begin your walk near the intersection of Silver Lake Boulevard and Glendale Boulevard. This is the heart of Mixville—the early filmmaking center where cowboy movie star Tom Mix lived and made westerns. (For years there was a bar at the corner of Brier Avenue and Glendale called The Mixer. Legend has it that Tom's horse is buried down the block, where the Ralph's supermarket stands now.) Depending on your mood and appetite, start with a light Vietnamese lunch at Gingergrass, a heavy German lunch at the Red Lion Tavern, or a cup of mud at the Silverlake Coffee Company. When you are sated, cross to the western side of Glendale (the reservoir side) and head south (or uphill).

As you go, note at 2379 Glendale the offices of Richard and Dion Neutra. They are the father and son architects—the only ones, I believe, with a Los Angeles street named after them—who built many of Silver Lake's signature homes. Richard labored under Frank Lloyd Wright and came to California to work with Rudolph Schindler before beginning his own empire. Dion later assumed the mantle after his father's death in 1970. Together, they are responsible for some of Los Angeles's most innovative homes.

To see a couple, turn right on Earl Street, walk down-hill, and view the first of the Neutra homes at 2434 Earl. Here, nestled in eucalyptus, is Dion's Treetops. Turn left immediately after onto Neutra Place to view a couple more classics, or continue straight on and turn left onto Silver Lake Blvd. Just ahead, at 2242, is Richard's Sokol House from 1948, the earliest and largest of the Neutra homes in the area.

About 100 yards on, turn left again and walk up a short stretch of Cove Avenue to the bottom of your first staircase.

This is a well-maintained set of stairs, 163 in all, poured by M.W. McCombs and inspected, like the Angelus steps (from Walk #24), by the delightfully-named "Rumble, City Inspector." It features no handrails, but is lined with laurel, oleander, bottlebrush, and wild grasses. Halfway up, the view of the reservoir is perfection. From here, you can also get a good look at the Landa staircase (from Walk #20) that offers equally breathtaking reservoir views from the other side.

At the top, pause to appreciate some local history: The house on your right, at 2328 Cove, is said to be the original 1950 meeting place of the Mattachine Society. Founded by transplanted Englishman Harry Hay, and including the fashion designer Rudi Gernreich in its membership, the society marked the beginning of the gay rights movement.

That done, continue along a block of charming two-story clapboard homes, and down the slope toward Glendale Blvd. At the bottom of the hill, cross Apex Avenue, and drop down a short flight of 19 stairs to land on Glendale itself.

Cross the boulevard—carefully!—and turn left. As you go, appreciate the steep incline of Edendale Place on your right. It is said that the hills in this area contain the steepest residential streets in the continental U.S. Be happy again that you are not a piano mover.

Turn right onto Loma Vista Place. Across Glendale, be-hind you, is a short set of public steps that used to connect to a pathway that ran between Cove and Earl. Now, they are just 62 steps going into someone's front yard.

Console yourself for that loss with a short walk up a steep stretch of Loma Vista, pausing at the top to appreciate the Anto-nio Gaudi-like wall, with its imaginative use of tile and rock, at 2384. I am told this home was designed by the "Pueblo Revival" architect Charles F. Whittlesey, who was also responsible for the famous Alvarado Hotel in Albuquerque, New Mexico, and the Livermore homes on Russian Hill in San Francisco.

The stairway just ahead might be the most delightful in the city. It is lined with small, attractive homes, and deeply shaded all the way along by ancient oak trees. The steps rise in comfortable stages with short walkways in between for a total of 182 paces. Along the way, there are delightful touches—the handmade mailboxes, the heavy-bag hanging from a gnarled eucalyptus tree, the scattering of children's toys in a garden, the tomato plants bursting in the sun. . . . A contractor's stamp in-dicates the stairs were poured in 1925 by C.W. Shafer.

At the top, the stairway narrows into a poorly maintained walkway. During a winter walk, I found a small landslide had closed one section down to a single pathway, but the last flight of stairs was of recent construction, with shiny new handrails.

Proceed down 50 yards of sloping walkway, to an even more deeply shaded section of stairs going down the backside of the Loma Vista walk-street. Here, the houses are more ram-shackle, but still charming. Some appear to have been left en-tirely alone since their construction almost 100 years ago. The overhang is a jungle of banana, palm, avocado, cedar, and pine trees, with explosions of bougainvillea covering some of the houses entirely. The stairs, when they arrive, are like a wide boulevard—twice the width of any other Silver Lake staircase. They total 69 stairs, and land on a two-lane walkway whose cen-ter divider is planted with very old jade and dracaena. Note the beautiful tiles and carved doorway at the big white house on the left as you continue your descent and finish the walk with one last set, across three landings, of 97 steps.

At the bottom, turn right onto Allesandro Way and walk a single block. To your left will be the Glendale Freeway and, past it, the hills of Echo Park. You might be able to spy the staircases rising up on Cove Ave. or Oak Glen Place—including a fine old wooden staircase from Walk #16.

These are for another day. Right now, turn right onto Oak Glen Place, and then right again onto Fair Oak View Terrace, then left at once, heading uphill, onto Edendale Place. (Unless you want to see a relic of bygone days. If you do, go left on Fair Oak View. About fifty yards up, on the left, you'll see a sign for Cove Ave., and some steps falling down toward the freeway. These used to connect to the old Red Car line as it headed for Edendale Station. Now they drop 48 steps into a wall of bush and bramble, and go nowhere at all.)

The Edendale stairs rise 134 steps, with handrails, up a green hillside pocked with little terraces and gardens. Over to your right, you can see the Loma Vista staircase you descended a few minutes earlier. Puff up to the top of the stairs, and at the top turn left into the alley. Then turn right again onto Edendale Place which will take you down the hill to Glendale Blvd. Turn right one last time, and walk along Glendale, back to your starting point.

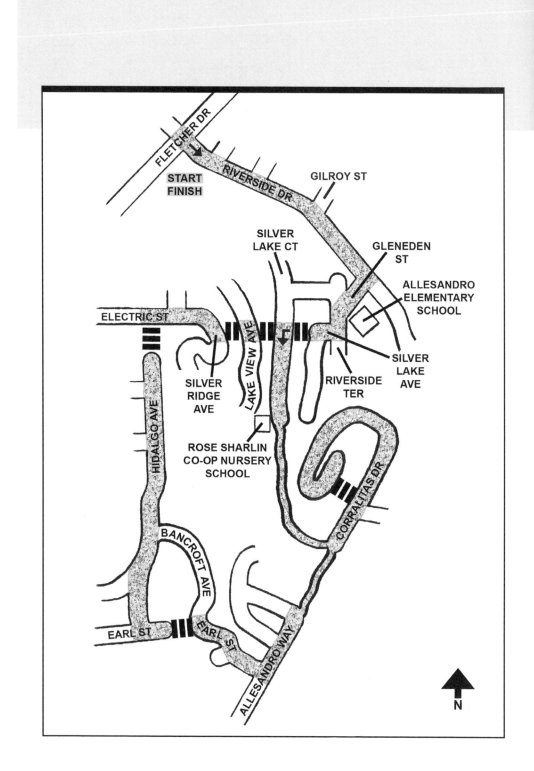

SILVER LAKE COURT
DURATION: **1 hour, 15 minutes**
DISTANCE: **3.2 miles**
STEPS: **603**
DIFFICULTY: **3.5**
BUS: **#96, 603**

This is a country walk in the city, along a stretch of the old Red Car electric trolley system. It has loads of elevation change, amazing views, and a bear hunt.

Begin your walk in Silver Lake, near the intersection of Riverside Drive and Fletcher Drive, perhaps with fries and a shake from Rick's or a used bicycle, book, or water ski from the quirky Coco's Variety Store. After equipping yourself, head east on Riverside, on the north side of the street, with the I-5 freeway close by on your left. As you approach the first traffic light, which is Gilroy Street, look at the hillside across Riverside. There's a cartoon bear painted onto the side of the hill, with the words "Found me!" next to it. Here's the bear hunt: Midway through this walk, if your eyes are sharp, you'll see a collection of four more identical bears. Find the bears, win a prize. (The answer is at the end of this walk.)

Cross the street at Gilroy, and continue along Riverside in the shade of the ramshackle houses clinging to the hillside above you. This isn't the most attractive part of the walk, but it doesn't last long. At the next corner, turn right onto Gleneden Street, just before you come to Allesandro Elementary School.

Go up a block and bear left, onto Riverside Terrace. Go one block more, and turn right onto Silver Lake Avenue.

Silver Lake *Avenue?* That can't be right. But it is. This isn't Silver Lake Boulevard, which runs on the eastern side of the reservoir, or West Silver Lake Drive, which runs on the western side. It's not connected to the *other* Silver Lake Boulevard, either—the one in Atwater Village, which is really confusing to people looking for addresses on that street. This is Silver Lake Avenue. It runs only two short blocks. Walk up these, and find your first staircase, going up.

This is an oddity. It's 30 steps, with a handrail but no lights, going *up* to an old transit line. Almost all the staircases in the city go *down,* from the hillsides to the transit lines, which tended to run in the canyons and flats. This flight goes up, and lands on Silver Lake Court.

This too is an oddity—a long, wide dirt road that is actually a piece of unincorporated land that used to be controlled by the public transit system. The old elevated Pacific Electric Red Car trolley line ran right through here, from Downtown Los Angeles out to Atwater Village, Glendale, and beyond. Just to the southeast was Edendale Station, and just in front of you was the India Street Station.

Across the dirt road, you will see a set of stairs going up. Ignore these, for now. Instead, turn left and follow the unpaved Silver Lake Ct. to its terminus, appreciating the views of Mt. Washington and the San Gabriel Mountains as you go. Near the end, you will sometimes see a surprising number of station wagons and minivans parked under the trees. This end of Silver Lake Ct. functions as an unofficial parking lot for Rose Scharlin Co-op Nursery School, whose backdoor is just up the hill to the right. Dating from 1939, it's one of the city's oldest educational institutions.

Just past the school, as the dirt road ends, walk straight ahead through a wide break in the foliage and enter a shady glade of pepper, eucalyptus, and black walnut trees. Note as you pass, a memorial garden, marked by a rock circle, to a fallen comrade.

Note also, a line of telephone poles up to the left. Beneath these was once a public staircase serving the Edendale Station.

Beyond that the path widens into a broad valley, which in springtime is generally hip-deep in wild mustard and anise. Follow the path across it, then head down and to the left and drop onto the paved cul-de-sac end of Corralitas Drive. Follow this 100 yards or so. Just at the turning for Rosebud Avenue, find your next staircase on the left.

This is a steep climb, 133 steps high over multiple landings, with a handrail at the bottom but none above that. Note the profusion of security cameras at the bottom. Connected to what? Placed by whom? It's anyone's guess. Pull yourself up to the top of the steps, gathering views of the Glendale Freeway, and beyond that, the west-facing hills of Echo Park. Hidden in the trees are Fellowship Parkway and the Paul Landacre cabin (described in detail in Walk #16).

Turn left, from the top of the stairs, and begin walking down a slight slope that bends to the right. Just past the house at 2598 Corralitas, behind a phalanx of trash barrels, you can find the remnants of that public staircase you saw earlier from the shady glade below. Still extant are 35 steps that end abruptly with a fence and a sharp drop. Down the road a bit farther, just past the house at 2586, you can see remnants of what might have been yet *another* set of stairs down to the Edendale Station. They are on private property now, and go nowhere.

Continue walking down and around Corralitas, which affords fine views of Glendale, Forest Lawn Memorial Park, and the mountains beyond. Gradually you will begin to see the Glendale Freeway again, and will find yourself back at the bottom of the Corralitas steps. The street is a corkscrew, and you've walked it back to its beginning.

Go straight ahead to the cul-de-sac end of the road and pick up a paved path running up the slope to your left, paralleling the freeway. At its end, step over the barricade onto the corner of Lake View Avenue and Allesandro Way. Just on your right is a big, square, white residence with a sign in the window reading "Holyland Exhibit." One of Silver Lake's hidden oddities, this is a Bible Knowledge Society museum dating from 1924, containing Middle Eastern antiquities including a mummy that predates Christ by 600 years. The museum is open to the public, but reservations are required.

Walk on by. Up and to your right, high on the hill, is another Middle Eastern oddity—a bright-white domed building that is actually a private home on the Loma Vista walk-street described in Walk #26. That's for another day. For now, walk two blocks to the corner of Earl Street and turn right.

Go up and around, ignoring the turning for Earl Court, and continue to the corner where Earl meets Bancroft Avenue. On the left is your next challenging staircase.

This one is a marvel of design and construction—courtesy of C.W. Shafer, inspected by W.E. Moyle—without rails or lights, but it's a numerologist's dream. Rising a total of 219 steps on a zigzag switchback pattern, this set comprises nine matching flights of 21 steps each, headed and footed by matched sets of 15 steps.

Halfway up, you are treated to majestic views of Echo Park, Mt. Washington, Mt. Wilson, and even, on clear days, Mt. Baldy, bright with snow in winter.

At the top, walk straight ahead, picking up views of the Silver Lake Reservoir and, on the other side of it, the sweeping driveway and roofline of architect John Lautner's Silvertop as you crest Earl St. To the left of that, and higher up, the old Canfield-Moreno Estate is buried in the dense trees. Somewhere in there, too, is the estate that once belonged to evangelist Aimee Semple McPherson, whose Foursquare Church is still an Echo Park feature.

Turn right at the first corner, and begin walking downhill on Hidalgo Avenue. As you go, the view widens to the west to include the hills of Los Feliz, the Hollywood sign, and the Griffith Observatory. Further along, the views move north, to include the broad green hillsides of Forest Lawn Memorial Park (where, indeed, Sister Aimee is interred beneath a block of lovely white marble) and the city of Glendale. Continue on Hidalgo past the intersection with Bancroft. As you approach 2335, pause. This is the house, designed in 1962 by Frank Lloyd Wright's grandson, Eric Lloyd Wright, for Rupert Pole, where Anaïs Nin lived and wrote the last years of her life. She died here in 1977. Just past the garage for the house at 2350, appreciate the old funicular railway on the right that used to ferry groceries and garbage cans up and down the steep hillside—one of many in the Silver Lake area.

Hidalgo drops and rises and drops again, past the turnings for Brier Avenue and Ayr Street. Continue straight on, cresting the final hill and finding the next set of stairs at the cul-de-sac end. On the curb are markings for 2470 and 2476. As you descend the stairs, you'll see the houses that belong to those addresses. The staircase, another C.W. Shafer construction, is a multiple-landing series of 82 steps, without rails or lights, dropping you down onto Electric Street. Turn right, and bear right at the turning for Silver Ridge Avenue. Up the slope a little, just where the curb marking reads 2494, take the next staircase—a set of 77 steps with a railing, but no lights—down onto Lake View Ave. Cross Lake View, and continue down the next set of stairs—a group of 31 interrupted by a sloping concrete walkway.

At the bottom, you'll find yourself once again back on the unpaved length of Silver Lake Ct. Cross the road, walk down the final 30 steps onto Silver Lake Ave., then turn left onto Riverside Terrace. Turn right down Gleneden, then turn left onto Riverside Dr. Walk straight down Riverside, back to Fletcher, and your starting point.

(Did you see the bears? They were painted onto the side of the house at 2517 Corralitas, as you rounded the corkscrew bend on your way down from the top of those stairs.)

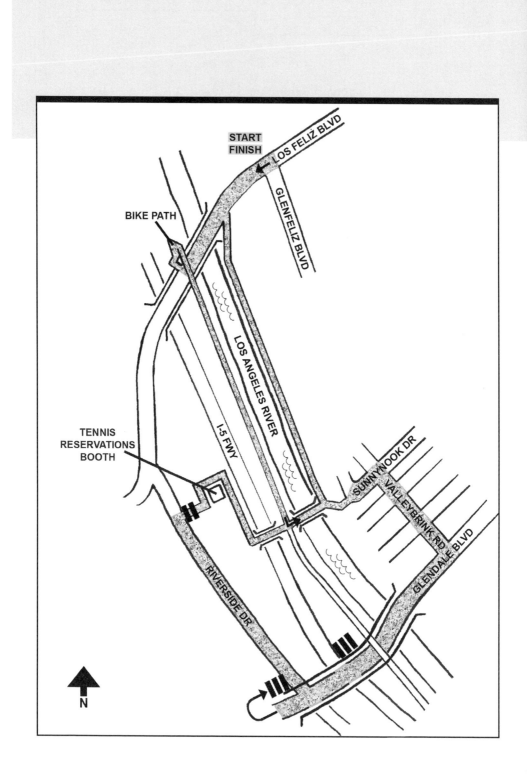

LOS ANGELES RIVER LOOP
DURATION: **1 hour, 15 minutes**
DISTANCE: **3 miles**
STEPS: **115**
DIFFICULTY: **2**
BUS: **#180, 181**

Here is a most unusual walk—a hybrid of gritty, urban stairs, and verdant, open wetlands. This relatively undemanding trek includes pedestrian bridges over freeways, secret paths through hobo camps, and the nesting habitats of exotic waterfowl. While not appropriate for everyone—women walking alone, children, hobo-phobes, and others—it offers a dramatic look at a seldom seen part of Los Angeles.

Start this walk in Atwater Village, just north of Griffith Park, perhaps with a burger from "EAT," also known as the Los Feliz Coffee Shop, at 3207 Los Feliz Boulevard. Begin by walking west on Los Feliz, toward the I-5 freeway, on the north side of the street. Just past the little 3-par golf course and the gated entrance to part of the riverside walkway, follow the sidewalk as it crosses the wide, concrete Los Angeles River. On the other side of the bridge, just before the freeway on-ramp, hook to the right and enter the bike path. After about 50 feet, make a U-turn, and follow the bike path as it rises up and over the Baum Bicycle Bridge. This will take you over Los Feliz Blvd. and deposit you on the Los Angeles River bike path.

The bike path is a relatively new construction—the bridge was built in 2002—that currently runs from the southern tip of Burbank all the way into Downtown Los Angeles. It's clean, lighted, and generally well maintained. It's also meant for bikes, so be careful as you walk to stay out of the way of the occasional passing cyclist.

Follow the river a few hundred feet and then, if you like, walk down the concrete embankment to the wide, flat section of walkway at the river's edge. (This is not advisable during wet weather, as the river's edge can be mossy and slippery. It is *never* advisable during rainy weather, as there is the risk of flash flooding.) Here, you will get a break from the freeway noise above and a front-row seat for some of the city's most remarkable water life. The pools and eddies here are home to great blue heron, snowy egret, black-necked stilt, and a variety of ducks and geese. Underwater are carp, catfish, and tilapia.

Return to the bike path as you approach the thin pedestrian bridge over the river, and then cross to the opposite bank. Once there, turn right onto the wide pathway, then left almost immediately just past the bench, dropping down the dirt path and landing on Sunnynook Drive. Walk up Sunnynook one block, and turn right onto Valley Brink Road—taking note of the corner house on your left and its remarkable flowing "grape arbor." Follow Valley Brink a couple of blocks until it butts into Glendale Blvd. Turn right onto Glendale.

Stick to the sidewalk and follow Glendale as it approaches the bridge and separates from Hyperion Avenue, crosses the river, and meets the bike path. Cross the freeway on-ramp here—*carefully*, because there is no crosswalk—and continue along the sidewalk. Just before it goes under the bridge, turn right and find your first staircase.

This is an elegant construction of 39 steps that sometimes also functions as a living room, restroom, and storage space for homeless people. Breathe through your mouth and step lively. At the top, turn right onto the bridge.

Even if you've never been here, you've been here. The

Glendale-Hyperion Viaduct was built in 1927 and has been featured in film and TV ever since. You may recognize the vintage lamps, octagonal turrets, or strategically-placed benches—not useful today, but probably very nice when the bridge was crossing a wide riverbed instead of the I-5 freeway—from noir movies of the 1940s. (The concrete waterway began construction in 1938, after a series of devastating floods cost dozens of lives and tens of millions of dollars in damage. Prior to that, it was open flood plain.) Behind you are good views of Atwater Village and, behind that, the wide lawns and ye olde English manor houses of Forest Lawn Memorial Park.

At the end of the bridge, make a buttonhook U-turn and take the second set of stairs, down this time over 62 steps, to land on Riverside Drive. Take a left, and follow the sidewalk to the first intersection. Cross Riverside at the crosswalk, and continue walking north. You'll pass Fellowship Auditorium on the right and, further ahead, you'll see the famous Mulholland fountain, where brides and grooms preen for wedding photographers on the weekends, their limos and proud parents standing nearby.

Stay on the north side of the street, though. Past the senior center and the parking lot, take the 14-step staircase that drops down to the tennis courts. Walk straight ahead, toward the "Tennis Reservations" booth. (There are public restrooms just to the right here.) Veer left, past the booth, and follow the sidewalk between the two sets of tennis courts. Turn right, where the courts end, and follow the dirt path behind the tennis courts to the back side of the soccer field. Here, the path turns left and rises onto a pedestrian bridge, this time carrying you up and over the I-5 freeway. You may pause and appreciate the strangely hypnotic effect of standing on top of 70 mph traffic.

When you've had enough of that, leave the bridge, cross the bike path and continue onto the pedestrian pathway over the Los Angeles River. Turn left on the other side this time, and follow the riverbank north. Here, the waterway is quieter, and the selection of waterfowl is more abundant. There are also benches and fitness stations, thanks to the efforts of Friends of the Los Angeles River, a non-profit organization founded in 1986 and dedicated to the restoration of this essential waterway. The green space before you, the trees, the bird habitat, and the lovely flowing water are all available for viewing largely due to FO-LAR's efforts, particularly the decades of commitment by local poet Lewis MacAdams. Pause here to give thanks, then continue along. As you go, you'll note wild grape vines, ancient agave plants, as well as bougainvillea, olive, and even fruit-bearing fig trees. Near the end of the asphalt walkway, take the dirt path to your right and follow it into a grove of sycamores, then onto the wide green lawn fronting Los Feliz Blvd. Bear right, and follow Los Feliz to the intersection with Glenfeliz Boulevard. You may end your walk here, with a fine Italian sandwich from Giamela's, a cocktail at the trendy Big Foot Lodge, or cross the street and return to EAT.

PART FOUR

HOLLYWOOD
AND LOS FELIZ

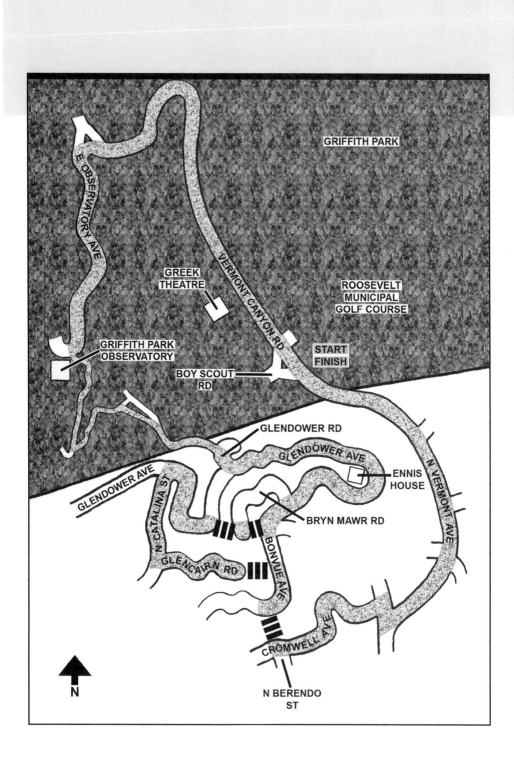

LOS FELIZ—GRIFFITH PARK LOOP
DURATION: **1 hour, 40 minutes**
DISTANCE: **3.8 miles**
STEPS: **463**
DIFFICULTY: **4.5**
BUS: **#180, 181, 780**

This is a challenging walk that rolls from the oak-lined foot-hills of Griffith Park up into the park itself, winding around the famed Griffith Observatory. Along the way, gigantic city views, some extreme staircases, and Frank Lloyd Wright.

Begin your walk at the Roosevelt Golf Course snack bar, situated just below the Greek Theatre, off Vermont Avenue about a half-mile above Los Feliz Boulevard. After a snack—I'll wager this is one of the few golf course coffee shops in America where you can get a steaming bowl of *kim chee chige* stew before waggling your niblick over the fairway—head south on Vermont Ave. Enjoy the spreading sycamore and coral trees, and stately gated homes, for about a third of a mile. Bear right, past Cockerham Drive, then turn right onto Cromwell Avenue and into a grove of oak trees. Wander west on this a bit, as the road rises and falls, continuing until the road meets N. Berendo Street. There, on your right, you will find your first set of stairs.

It's a significant staircase, built in 1924 by contractor C.H. Johnston, and is one of the very few to be granted historical status by the City of Los Angeles. It features beautiful brickwork and a plaque declaring that it owes its protected status largely to one Paul Rudnicki, "who gave this project life." The climb is without handrails, but the designers placed benches at the bottom, in the middle, and at the top. You may need them: It's 181 steps in all, well tended and neat, and shaded and cool, even in hot weather.

At the top, landing at about 4800 Bonvue Avenue, enjoy the benches or turn right and begin walking up the hill. Don't walk far. Keep your eye on the opposite side of the street, and look for the house at 4781. Just past it, underneath a giant, gnarled eucalyptus, you will find a very discreet set of public stairs on the left.

This feels like a private stairway, hugging close to the house on the left. It rises 70 steps—wide and well maintained, but without handrails or lights, past a stamp indicating it is another work of C.H. Johnston—and emerges through an arched gate between a house and its garage. You will land at the cul-de-sac ending of Glencairn Road. Walk straight ahead, out of the cul-de-sac, and head downhill. Along the way, you may enjoy the Moorish structure at 4840 with a peculiarly indefinite statue in its yard—A cat? A dog? A catdog?—and the corrugated steel box across the street from it. Just beyond is a vacant lot lending great city views.

Glencairn will meet N. Catalina Street. Bear right and head uphill, to where Catalina meets Glendower Avenue, and bear right again and head uphill some more. On your left, you may see trails leading into Griffith Park and up toward the observatory. On your right, you will obtain even better views of Hollywood and Downtown Los Angeles.

Further on, at the crest of the hill, you will find another rarity: A sign on the right indicating a staircase, which reads "Public Walk." It is battered and has a distinctly 1930s Raymond Chandler feel to it—you can imagine Philip Marlowe leaning against it, watching the city below, encased in misty rain, musing over the beastliness of his fellow miscreants. Take the indicated staircase, down a steep 133 steps, pausing at intervals to admire the fine Frank Lloyd Wright Ennis House crouched like a melting Mayan ruin, off to your left. You land on the cul-de-sac end of Bryn Mawr Road. Cross the street, and continue down another 79 steps—past a tiled mural featuring highlights of Hollywood—and drop down to Bonvue.

From here, you could take the short way home, going right down Bonvue and taking the Berendo steps down to the left. Or you could take an even shorter way home, crossing the street and picking up Glendower as it goes downhill. Either way would lead you back to Cromwell, back to Vermont, and back to the golf course.

But why cheat yourself? Instead, turn left and head up-hill on Glendower. Wander up and around. On your right you will pass the charming "Witches' Whimsy," a 1920s cottage said to have been designed to mimic the original Tam O'Shanter Inn in Atwater Village. Shortly after, the Ennis House will show it-self on your left. Continue up, winding around the great Frank Lloyd Wright building, until you come to its front.

This remarkable textile-block house from 1924 is one of the master's masterpieces, and has been featured in Hollywood films from *Day of the Locust* to *Bladerunner*. It mirrors and faces, down and across the valley below you, the equally magnificent Hollyhock House at Barnsdall Park. Said to have been inspired in part by the great Mayan temple at Uxmal, in Mexico, the En-nis House is also rumored to be on the market. The Ennis House Foundation, having already overseen a massive, decades-long resurrection of the house, determined it could no longer afford its upkeep. They put the house up for sale in 2009, at an asking price of $15 million. They also advised any prospective owners that an additional $10 million in repair bills could be anticipat-ed over the next 10 years or so.

Continuing on, rising still, you will eventually find a turning on the right for Glendower Rd. Take it to its end, about a city block on, and walk through the gates into Griffith Park.

You will be on a fire road, leading past an old 1950s air raid warning signal on the right, that offers staggering views of Hollywood and beyond on the left—all the way to Santa Monica, the Pacific Ocean, and even Catalina Island on clear days. Where the paved road splits, you may head to the right and catch the wide-paved dirt path going downhill, to emerge onto Boy Scout Rd. just in front of the golf course coffee shop.

But press on! Bear left instead. Soon the pavement will end and a dirt road will continue. Turn left when you meet a wider trail, still rising up as you go. When you come to the hairpin right turn at the base of the Observatory, enjoy the amazing views from Downtown to the beach, make the hard right and continue up the last steep part of the trail.

At last you will arrive at the front of the famous Griffith Observatory, where James Dean, Natalie Wood, and Sal Mineo acted out the dramatic conclusion to *Rebel Without a Cause*. If you are in need of education about the solar system, you might duck into the building and brush up on your retrograde orbits. If you are in need of more earthly sustenance, there is a Wolfgang Puck café on the far side of the building.

Otherwise, bear right past the lawn, and take the road heading downhill. This is East Observatory Avenue. It will lead you shortly past a small triangular traffic island. Up and to the left is the tunnel through which Roger Rabbit transitioned between the real world and Toon Town in the 1988 film, *Who Framed Roger Rabbit*. Down and to the right, you continue back onto Vermont Canyon Road. Head down the canyon, past the bird sanctuary on the left and a vintage public restroom over on your right. Beyond that is the Greek Theatre. A little farther along, on the opposite side, you will find the golf course, the coffee shop, and the end of this walk.

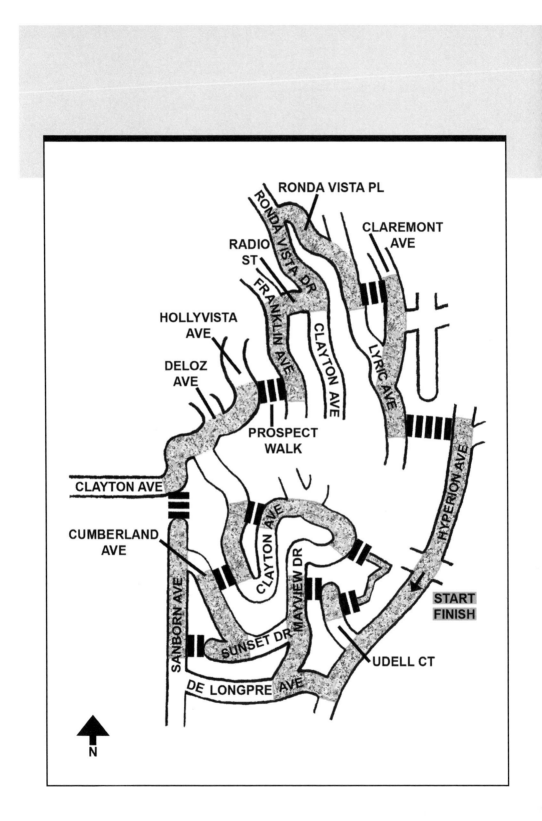

FRANKLIN HILLS EAST—LYRIC LOOP
DURATION: **1 hour**
DISTANCE: **2.9 miles**
STEPS: **908**
DIFFICULTY: **4**
BUS: **#175**

This is an energetic walk up, down, and around the hill separating East Hollywood from West Silver Lake, and includes some of the best hidden staircases in Los Angeles. Along the way are architectural peculiarities and fantastic views.

Begin your walk on Hyperion Avenue, near the corner of Lyric Avenue—perhaps at the Lyric-Hyperion Theater and Café on the corner. Cross to the west side of Hyperion and walk south, or downhill. Observe the good-looking Moderne building at 2035 Hyperion—a 1939 Robert Cassidy design—and the unmarked, but very trendy, Hyperion Tavern at 1941. Turn right at the second corner, onto De Longpre Avenue. Turn right again at the next corner, and begin walking uphill on Mayview Drive. Halfway up the hill, take the first flight of stairs—39 steps, going down to Udell Court.

Turn right onto Udell and head downhill, past a line of little wooden houses. Just at 3838 Udell, take the almost-hidden set of steps on the left. Climb up—appreciating the tin-roof siding and golden cherubs on the right, and the odd garden on the left—a total of 111 steps. Walk straight ahead on the concrete walkway. Across the Hyperion gulch, you might catch glimpses of the Landa steps or the Drury steps (which are part of Walks #20 and #21, respectively). Observe also the plastic chairs caged in chain link, which must be someone's private sunset viewing area.

At the end of the walkway, hook left and climb the 96 steps, past the small artists' studios on your right. At the top, step out at 2040 Mayview and turn right.

Wind up and around. At the next intersection, bear left onto Clayton Avenue. Halfway down the block, just before 3819, take the short flight of 10 steps up and 27 steps down, to land on the other side of the Clayton loop. Turn left, and walk to the house at 3884 Clayton. Take this nicely hand-railed set of 61 steps going down to an elbow in the staircase. Note the dolphin fountain on the right, then continue down 65 steps more to land at 3949 Cumberland Avenue.

Turn left. Follow Cumberland around to the hairpin right at Sunset Drive. Take the right, and walk to the end of the Sunset Dr. cul-de-sac, then take the 43 steps down onto Sanborn Avenue.

Turn right onto Sanborn. Follow this, again, to its cul-de-sac end, ignoring the "Dead End" sign. Appreciate the faux castle at 1560 Sanborn, then drop down 41 steps to land back on another stretch of Clayton Ave. Turn right, and begin marching uphill. Follow Clayton to the first intersection, and turn left onto Deloz Avenue, then turn right almost immediately onto Hollyvista Avenue. Continue uphill, and at 1800 Hollyvista, take the stairs known as Prospect Walk.

This is a nice climb, with good handrails on both sides, up 168 steps. You land, huffing and puffing, at 3814 Franklin Avenue. Turn left. Follow Franklin to where it meets the paved section of Radio Walk—another monumental set of stairs, covered in detail in Walk #31—and turn right. Go one block, and turn left onto Ronda Vista Drive. At the next corner, hook right onto Ronda Vista Place—pausing to admire the very nice Japanese stone lantern at 3835. (There is sometimes a car parked here that is coated entirely in computer keyboard keys. That's worth a look, too.) Drop down the hill to meet Lyric Ave., and bear right.

Just after 2346 Lyric, find the nearly invisible staircase by the yellow hydrant. This is a messy, often overgrown walkway that falls 110 steps down to Claremont Avenue. Turn right and walk slightly uphill past Entrance Drive, to merge with Lyric once more. Continue along and find the next well-hidden staircase just past 2232 Lyric. This is the Scotland staircase, and your final set of steps for the day. Drop down 137 steps—pausing to observe the locked set of stairs that once connected this staircase to the cul-de-sac end of Tracy Terrace—to land on Hyperion once more. Turn right. Walk the long block back to the corner of Lyric—appreciating as you go the peculiar architecture of 2220 Hyperion, which used to be a Safeway supermarket but is now a business office for a food and drug industry union. Just ahead is the end of your walk.

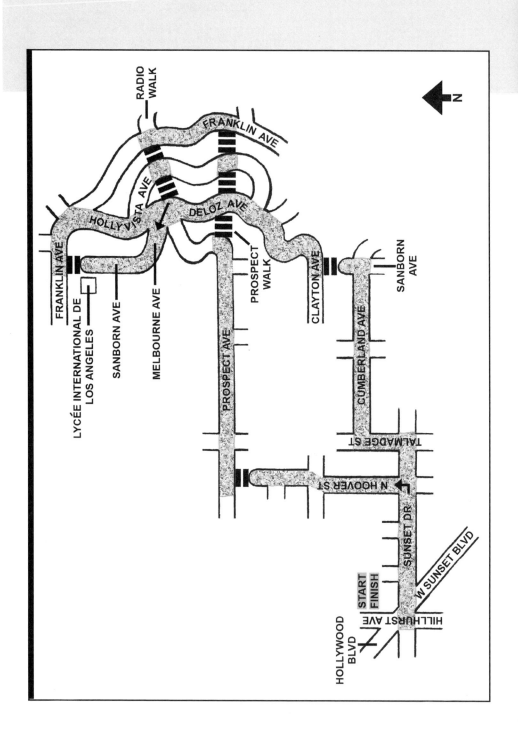

FRANKLIN HILLS WEST—
RADIO-PROSPECT LOOP
DURATION: **1 hour**
DISTANCE: **2.7 miles**
STEPS: **684**
DIFFICULTY: **4**
BUS: **#2, 26, 302**

Here's a relatively short, but demanding, East Hollywood hike, with lots of elevation change—a serious workout for the calves and quads. It includes stretches of two of the city's few officially designated walk-streets, Radio Walk and Prospect Walk.

Begin this walk from the complicated intersection where Hollywood Boulevard, Sunset Boulevard and Hillhurst Avenue meet, with a coffee at Café at the Vista or a movie at the Vista itself—where the footprints of the stars belong not to cinema celebrities but to indie movie directors like Penelope Spheeris, Allison Anders, and Jon Favreau. When you're done, walk east on Sunset Drive—*not* Sunset Blvd.—and head for the hills. Walk past the back entrance to El Chavo Mexican restaurant, and the backside of public broadcast station KCET. Cross Rosalia Road and N. Commonwealth Avenue, and then turn left onto Hoover Street. One block up, jog slightly to the right, and continue up Hoover. At the end of the next block, find your first staircase.

This is "Hoover Walk," a lovely double-sided staircase, dating from 1923 and adorned with marvelous murals. Climb up

38 steps, and turn right onto Prospect Avenue. Cross Talmadge Street, with the ABC-operated Prospect Studio on your left. This is real old Hollywood. The production facility opened in 1915 as the Vitagraph Studio, before Warner Bros. bought the property in 1925 and made movies there—among them, part of its first "talkie," *The Jazz Singer*—until it sold the soundstages to ABC in 1948. Ernie Kovacs shot his short-lived TV show here, as did the producers of *Family Feud*, *General Hospital*, *Grey's Anatomy*, and dozens of other familiar TV series.

Continuing on Prospect, you'll pass Myra Avenue and Sanborn Avenue, and begin your ascent. Just past the house at 3976, as the road begins a blind curve to the left, find your next staircase on the right.

This is the bottom of Prospect Walk, as proclaims a sign often hidden in the unpruned trees. It's a nice shady run of 57 steps without rails or lights that lifts you up to Deloz Avenue. Cross the street, and continue onto the walk's middle section. This one features 71 steps, again without rails or lights, and carries you up to Hollyvista Avenue. Cross the street again, and press on! The last stage is 168 steps, up multiple sections, without lights but with a handrail. It drops you at 3814 Franklin Avenue, possibly quite winded, at the top of Franklin Hills.

Turn left, and try to find the "Prospect Walk" sign hanging from the elegant old lamppost—if you can find the lamppost. Both are usually hidden by the fiddle leaf fig tree growing around them. When you've caught your breath, begin walking downhill on Franklin.

After a bit, you'll come to a turning to the right. This is the road section of Radio Walk. Ignore that, but look to the left for the Radio Walk staircase. Stop to appreciate the huge western views here—of Hollywood, the Sunset Strip, Century City, and beyond. Then begin the descent.

Radio Walk comes in two sections. The first is a steep, quadricep-challenging drop of 127 steps that lands you on Hollyvista once more. Cross the street and take the next section, which drops 97 more steps down to Deloz.

Directly ahead is Prospect Avenue. Just to the right is Melbourne Avenue. Head for that, enjoying a block of modest homes and welcome shade, until Melbourne bends to the right and turns into Sanborn. Admire on the left the playing fields and gardens of LILA—the Lycée International de Los Angeles, a bilingual French-English K-12 school founded in 1978. Follow the LILA fence to the end of Sanborn. There on the left you'll find your next staircase.

It's marked with a smart-looking contractor's stamp declaring it the 1926 work of Robert Metcalf. It has no rails or lights, but is a nicely symmetrical set of 85 wide steps carrying you up to Franklin Ave.

To the left is the charming Shakespeare Bridge, also a 1926 construction, spanning 260 feet and adorned with peculiar Gothic guard towers. Admire this, and then turn back to the right and head uphill. Pass the fine looking mid-century home at 3959—prominently featured in the 2009 comedy *I Love You, Man*—and bear right, heading downhill onto Hollyvista. Dig the Tara-like structure at 2018, as Hollyvista winds around and down. Bear right again onto Deloz. Pass the Radio Walk steps to your left—or, for a *big* workout, run up the steps, turn right onto Franklin, then run down the Prospect Walk steps and rejoin the walk there.

Otherwise, go straight ahead on Deloz, up and over the small rise, past the lower and middle sections of Prospect Walk and the turning for Hollyvista. At the corner, turn right and head downhill on Clayton Avenue.

There are very good views on the right side of Griffith Park, the Observatory, and the Hollywood sign. There may also be good views of *you*: check out the security cameras at 3951.

Follow Clayton down and around. Just as the road completes a big bend to the right, find the final staircase on your left. This is a short sweep of 41 steps, with a rail but no lights, that carries you up to the cul-de-sac end of Sanborn Ave. Walk along Sanborn, not missing the dimpled castle on the left at 1560. At the stop sign, turn right and descend onto Cumberland Avenue.

Here is the last of your quad exercises. Drop down, past Myra, observing the little worker cottages on both sides of the street, built 100 years ago or more, probably for the Vitagraph Studios employees. Make a short climb to Talmadge Street, turn left, and at the stop sign turn right onto Sunset Dr. and continue back to your starting point.

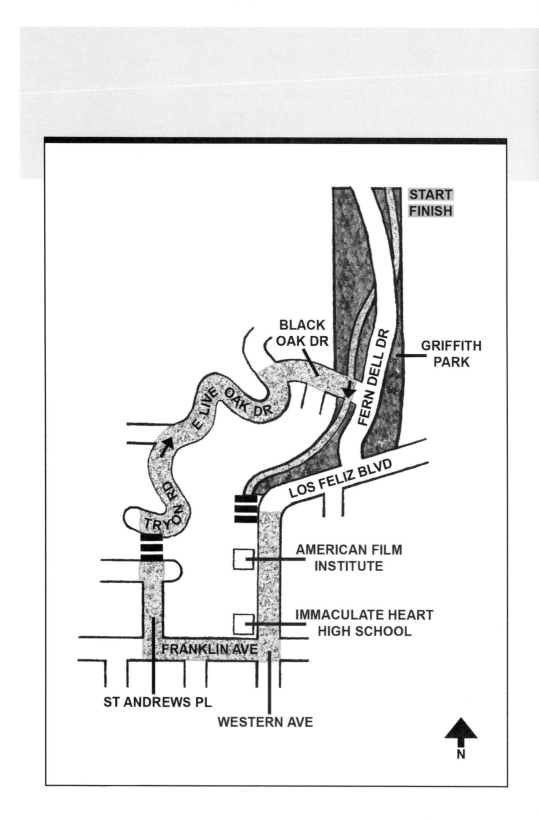

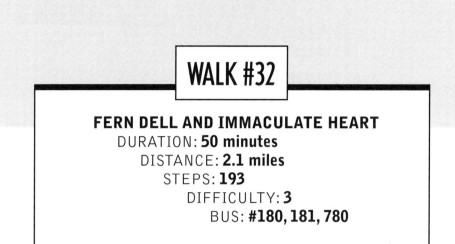

WALK #32

FERN DELL AND IMMACULATE HEART
DURATION: **50 minutes**
DISTANCE: **2.1 miles**
STEPS: **193**
DIFFICULTY: **3**
BUS: **#180, 181, 780**

Here's a great hot day walk along a cool, shady creek, past a venerable educational institution, then up a grand staircase of historical importance—all in the middle of Hollywood.

Begin your walk at the western-most edge of Griffith Park, near where Los Feliz Boulevard meets Western Avenue. Park just above Los Feliz on Fern Dell Drive, across from The Trails Café, and walk downhill on the east side of the street, entering Fern Dell.

This is a charming, very un-Los Angeles promenade, a creekside walk through the strangest mix of flora. There are redwoods and banana trees, palms and pines, and ferns and hanging bromeliads, all landscaped into a winding, shady canyon and fitted out with pleasant benches and well-maintained walkways, lined with Disney-esque *faux bois* handrails. Follow the creek as it wanders under Fern Dell Dr. and emerges on the west side. Stay with it until the walkway ends, then exit through the black iron gates onto the intersection of Fern Dell and Black Oak Drive. Turn right onto Black Oak, then left immediately onto the asphalt path running along the shoulder of the park, toward Los Feliz Blvd.

This will lead you past a fine-looking house that calls it-self "High Trilling Manor," and past an old wooden Craftsman home that calls itself "Hodges Station." The first is a private home. The second is an outbuilding connected to the American Film Institute, the campus of large white buildings that will gradually be visible on your right. Just after Hodges Station, you'll find the first set of stairs, a wide sweeping staircase over several landings that drops 40 paces down to land you on Western Ave.

The quiet of Fern Dell gone, follow Western down to Franklin Avenue, passing Immaculate Heart High School. (The Catholic organization used to operate a university here, too, in the buildings that now house AFI. Sister Corita Kent, the artist/activist whose "Love" poster was a 1960s visual icon, ran the art department.) Turn right, past the school, onto Franklin. Walk one noisy block down Franklin, and turn right at the first corner, onto St. Andrews Place.

At the top of the first leafy block, an enormous home will appear on the left. Directly beside it, straight ahead of you, is the second staircase.

This is a massive set of stairs, rising 153 steps over multiple stages, with benches along the way and a beautiful arched patio at the halfway point. It is also in terrible disrepair—bottles, graffiti, cigarette butts, and beer cans—evidence of a city that has no sense of pride and a populace that has no sense of shame. Despite the debris, there are lovely views of Downtown Los Angeles and downtown Hollywood. Overlook the mess, and climb the second steep section to land at 5680 Tryon Road. Turn right, and head uphill.

The crenellated castle at 5647 is said to have been home to Nicolas Cage. The fine Spanish at 5630 looks like it might have been part of Immaculate Heart at one point in time. As you pass these and climb, you'll get good views straight down onto the top of AFI. Continue climbing, and at the stop sign, turn right and head downhill on East Live Oak Drive. Admire the good-looking Japanese "tea house" on the left and note, on the right, the back side of Hodges Station. At the first corner, turn right onto Black Oak Dr., slowing to appreciate the recently renovated and strikingly beautiful Lloyd Wright (son of Frank Lloyd) home—rising from the cactus garden like a Mayan temple—on the left, at 2158 West Live Oak.

Black Oak will lead you back down to Fern Dell. Re-enter the park through the black iron gates, and follow the creek back up to The Trails Café, and the end of this walk.

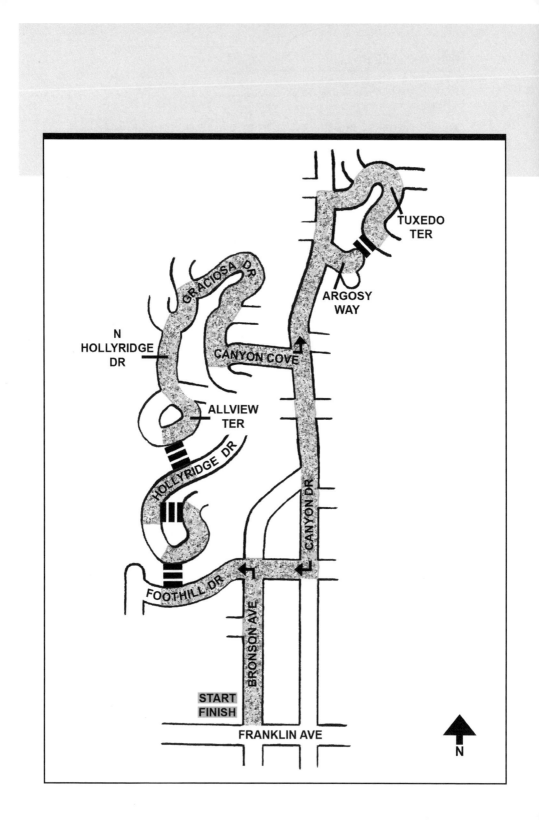

TUXEDO
TER

GRACIOSA DR

N
HOLLYRIDGE
DR

ARGOSY
WAY

CANYON COVE

ALLVIEW
TER

HOLLYRIDGE DR

CANYON DR

FOOTHILL DR

BRONSON AVE

START
FINISH

FRANKLIN AVE

N

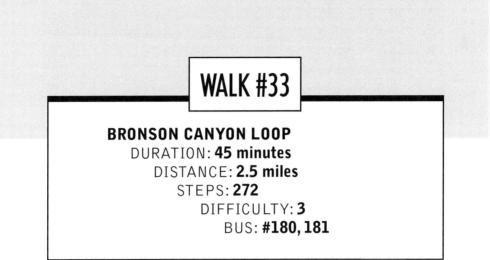

WALK #33

BRONSON CANYON LOOP
DURATION: **45 minutes**
DISTANCE: **2.5 miles**
STEPS: **272**
DIFFICULTY: **3**
BUS: **#180, 181**

This is a gentle, deeply shaded hillside walk along hidden staircases, featuring interesting old Los Angeles architecture and great views of Hollywood, the Hollywood Hills, and Griffith Park.

Begin your walk in Hollywood, near the corner of Franklin Avenue and Bronson Avenue, perhaps with a breakfast at Victor's, on the west side of Bronson, or a snack from Gelson's, across the street. As you digest, make your way north on Bronson. Watch for good examples of clapboard-sided Craftsman homes, and signs reading "No Access to the Hollywood Sign"— themselves a sign of local residents irritated by tourists trying to get to the historic landmark. Two blocks north of Franklin, turn left onto Foothill Drive.

On your left are good views of downtown Hollywood. On the right is the first of this walk's signature homes—a large Spanish bearing the name "Villa Maria" over the door. Just afterward, at 5941 Foothill, you'll come to a garden decorated with a collection of lovely blue-glass bottles. At the end of the garden, find the first staircase, on the right, heading up. Take the 62 steps to the top, and land at 2241 Hollyridge Drive.

Directly across the street is the second of this walk's signature homes—another Spanish, even larger, bearing the name
"Belvedere." Turn right, admiring the estate's sloping lawns and
fine Florida and Royal palms, and head down the hill and around
the corner. Just past the house at 2200 Hollyridge, you'll find the
next staircase, on your left.

This is a dark, cool, heavily shaded set of stairs, rising
72 steps over several landings, tight between two houses. At the
top, you land back on Hollyridge. Turn right, and head uphill,
past the driveway on your right for the private enclave of Hollyridge Park. Just after the house at 2325, on your left, find the
next stairs—another deeply shaded set, rising 87 paces, that lifts
you onto Allview Terrace East. Turn right, and circle around to
the intersection where Allview Terrace East meets Allview Terrace West, and turn right. Immediately after, bear left back onto
Hollyridge Dr.

The houses here are an amusing hodge-podge of styles,
from Italianate and overbearing to English Tudor and understated. Continue along, bearing right at the next intersection,
turning onto Graciosa Drive. At the next corner, observe the
curious wagon-wheel eaves and conical witch-hat roof at 2478,
and turn right again, following Graciosa down and around as it
loops back toward Bronson Canyon. Note the strange "heads"
and metal sculptures in the garden at 5963. Continue straight
on as Graciosa turns into Manola Way, then take the hard left
onto Canyon Cove. At the bottom of the hill, where you meet
Canyon Drive, cross the street and turn left.

If you were to continue to the end, you would find some
very good mountain hiking trails. For now, though, walk two
blocks to Argosy Way and turn right. Head uphill, bearing left
at the Y-intersection, find your final staircase at the end of the
cul-de-sac. It sits next to the house at 2424, and rises very dis-
creetly through deep shade, 51 steps up to land on the charmingly named Tuxedo Terrace. Turn left, and head downhill, appreciating again another stretch of good shade and a selection
of amusing architectural styles. Stay on the left past the turning

for Cazaux Drive, heading always downhill, until you meet Canyon Dr. again. Turn left, and retrace your steps back down the canyon.

A few blocks on, at 2217, you'll see the last of the walk's signature houses, this time the Villa Enriqueta, a large shingle-sided home fronted by freestone walls. Just ahead, at the fork where N. Bronson Ave. peels off to the right, continue straight, staying on Canyon Dr. On the left, you'll see large security gates preventing you from entering the "private" street of Valley Oak Drive. Behind those gates, among other things, is the compound of several houses where Brad Pitt and Angelina Jolie make their home in Los Angeles.

At the next intersection, turn right onto Foothill. After one block, turn left onto Bronson Ave. Follow Bronson back to your starting point, and the end of this walk.

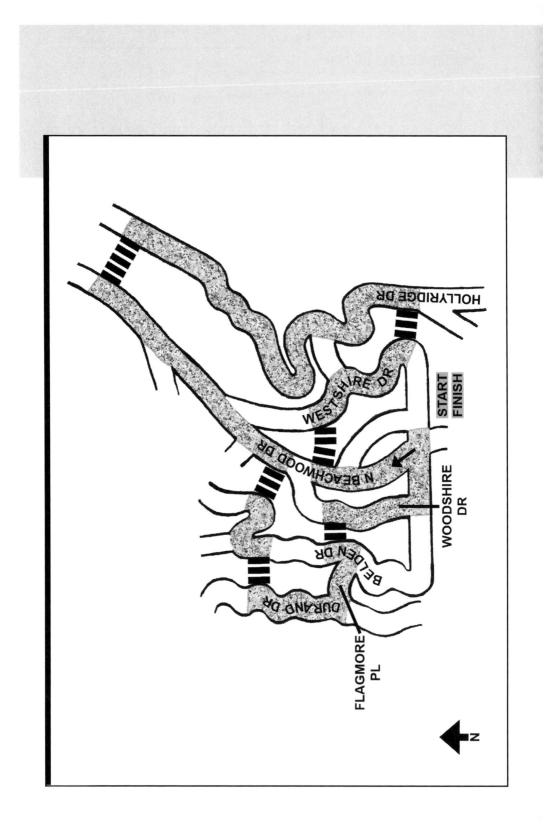

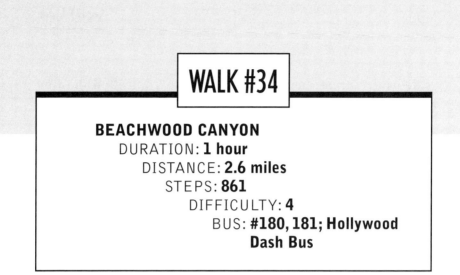

BEACHWOOD CANYON
DURATION: **1 hour**
DISTANCE: **2.6 miles**
STEPS: **861**
DIFFICULTY: **4**
BUS: **#180, 181; Hollywood Dash Bus**

This is a vigorous hike through Hollywood history, utilizing some of the steepest and most charming staircases in the city, and affording breathtaking views from Downtown to the sea.

Begin your walk up Beachwood Canyon, near the Village Coffee Shop at 2695 N. Beachwood Drive, just beyond the stone arches built to celebrate the creation of Hollywoodland. This was one of Hollywood's first premier housing schemes, organized by a consortium of men including Harry Chandler, of the *Los Angeles Times*, and General M.H. Sherman, after whom Sherman Oaks is named. It was intended as a gated community—hence those arches—with tennis courts, swimming pools, and riding stables for its well-heeled residents. (These would include, over time, Busby Berkeley, Humphrey Bogart, Bela Lugosi, Bugsy Siegel, and many others.) To advertise the scheme, the consortium built a huge sign reading "Hollywoodland," framed in thousands of light bulbs. The mountainside calling card became more famous after the "land" part fell off and left behind the "Hollywood" known around the world.

Start walking due north on Beachwood Dr., on the right

side of the street. Just after the house at 2800, find the first staircase going up. This is an elegant, shaded set of very steep stairs, cut from the same granite as the stone Hollywoodland gates, rising a sharp 143 steps to Westshire Drive. Take a right, climb a little more, then bear right, and follow Westshire as it loops downhill. Just after 2748 Westshire on the left, take the next set of stairs going up.

These are even steeper and shadier than the previous set, complemented by nice wrought iron handrails, rising 149 steps—the last 84 in a single unbroken run. Land panting at the top on Hollyridge Drive, and turn left.

Across the way is the crenellated wall of a faux Hollywood castle. Up ahead, following Hollyridge along the ridge, there is a hidden elevator inside the tower at 2922. Further along, another crenellated wall up to the right announces yet another fake castle—the hills are full of them.

Just after 3057 Hollyridge, find the more recently constructed staircase to the left. This is a rapid drop of 178 steps, through shaded backyards, very narrow but with double handrails, that lands you at 3020 N. Beachwood Dr. Take a left, and head downhill. Admire the very odd Prince Valiant mural on the front of 2925—complete with archer's bow and falcon. At the corner of N. Beachwood and Woodshire Drive, locate the next set of stairs.

This is the granddaddy of Beachwood stairs, a towering double set separated by a stone wall that used to contain a running stream. Now it holds planter boxes and, further up, provides useful benches for resting. At the bottom is a plaque, declaring the staircase Historic-Cultural Monument No. 535 and giving its date of construction as 1928. Mull that over as you march up 148 very steep steps, perhaps pausing to enjoy one of the benches as you go.

Turn left at the top and follow Belden Drive around a couple of bends. Then find the walkway on the right, just before the house at 2917, marked by a pair of white wooden posts. Between the houses is the bottom of the next staircase—another set of granite steps, again with fine wrought iron handrails, charging up 118 individual risers to the top. Land at 2954 Durand Drive, and take a left.

Walk down and around, enjoying views of the Hollywood sign behind you, the Griffith Observatory to your left, and downtown Hollywood straight ahead. As Durand drops and passes the left hand turning for Flagmoor Place, take a little detour and continue up the other side of Durand. On your right is the granite wall, reminiscent of the parapets at Le Mont-Saint-Michel, of Wolf's Lair—a three-acre Norman-style chateau, complete with heart-shaped swimming pool and a guesthouse designed by famed Silvertop architect John Lautner. For sale in 2009 for $7.5 million, the house feels very Errol Flynn, but is said to have been home to film star Debbie Reynolds and *The View* star Debbie Matenopoulos. It was originally built for L. Milton Wolf, one of Hollywoodland's original investors.

At the hairpin corner, which is the intersection of Durand and the unpaved fire road section of Mulholland Drive, enjoy a fine view of Lake Hollywood. You can extend your walk by taking Mulholland down and around to the reservoir itself.

Trot back down Durand, turn right on Flagmoor, and turn left again onto Belden. Walk up one short stretch, and look for the amusing sign saying "Slow. Adults at Play." It features a jolly party animal, clutching a wine bottle. Just after the house at 2872, find your final staircase, another granite set with wrought iron rails, dropping 125 steps down to Woodshire. Enjoy the Antonio Gaudi/Simon Rodia-style bottle-walls on your left as you go. And, at the bottom, witness a profusion of amateur artwork. To the left is a pair of topiary rabbits. Straight across is a totem-pole garage door design. Turn right, down Woodshire, and follow it until it meets Belden. Turn left and walk to Beachwood, and the end of this walk.

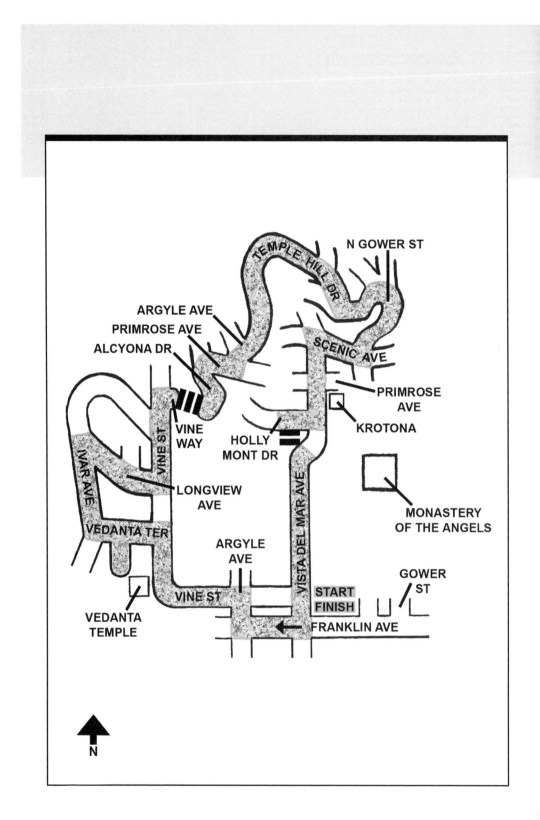

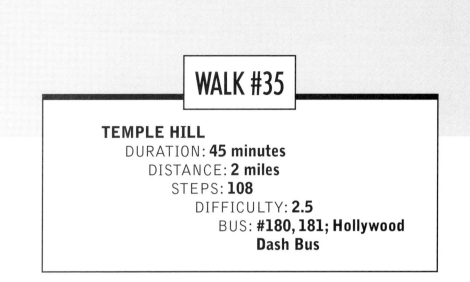

TEMPLE HILL
DURATION: **45 minutes**
DISTANCE: **2 miles**
STEPS: **108**
DIFFICULTY: **2.5**
BUS: **#180, 181; Hollywood Dash Bus**

This is a most spiritual walk, a hillside stroll without too many stairs through an area once dotted with temples, monasteries, retreats, and church buildings. The English novelist Christopher Isherwood studied meditation here; the Indian spiritualist Krishnamurti lived here; and the Dominican sisters still bake a mean pumpkin bread here.

Begin your walk in Hollywood, near the corner of Franklin Avenue and Vista Del Mar Avenue, perhaps with breakfast at the 101 Coffee Shop, the hipster hangout featured in the comedy *Swingers*. Start walking west on Franklin, noticing as you go the recently renovated Hollywood Tower Apartments on your left and, as you meet Argyle Avenue and turn right, the Castle Argyle Apartments on your right. At the base of the apartments, turn left and head up the slope of Vine Street.

As the slope flattens and bends left, you enter the Hollywood Dell residential section—a section that stretches to near the John Anson Ford Amphitheatre. Follow Vine up to the corner, and turn left on Vedanta Terrace. Take a left again onto Vedanta Place.

This lovely spot is the Southern California home of the Vedanta Society, a sect founded by the 19th-century Indian ascetic Ramakrishna. His disciple Swami Vivekananda was sent to America to spread the word, and *his* follower Swami Prabhavananda founded the Hollywood location. Among his followers was the English prose stylist Christopher Isherwood, whose book *My Guru and His Disciple* chronicles his apprenticeship. The temple still functions as a monastery, as well as a meditation center, and is open to the public. (There are other Vedanta centers in San Diego, Santa Barbara, and South Pasadena.)

Retrace your steps to Vedanta Terrace, turn left, and then turn right onto Ivar Avenue. Climb Ivar to the corner, and turn right on Longview Avenue. There, at the corner, enjoy the faux chateau at 2062. Continue along Longview, past Mound Street, and then turn left back onto Vine.

The surrounding blocks are full of early Hollywood history. The big Italian structure at 2027 was home to Jeanette MacDonald, the musical film actress probably best known for singing the title song in the 1936 movie *San Francisco*. Across the street, Charlie Chaplin was once a resident at what is now the Monastery Gardens Apartments. Down the block, cowboy star Hopalong Cassidy lived in the big Spanish adobe at 2030.

Head uphill on Vine, past the Monastery Gardens. At the next corner, turn right onto Vine Way. At the end of the cul-de-sac—by the house at 6382, designed by Richard Neutra acolyte Gregory Ain—find your first staircase.

This is a delightful winding set of 47 steps, with a rail, but no lights, from contractor C.H. Johnston. It drops you at 2300 Alcyona Drive. Head uphill, past the lovely spreading oak at 2122, and turn right at the next corner, onto the steep stretch of Primrose Avenue. At the top of the rise, turn left onto Argyle, and then veer right at once onto Temple Hill Drive.

The surrounding neighborhood was once home to a profusion of spiritual centers. Principal among them was Krotona, the Southern California headquarters of the Eastern-influenced Theosophical Society from 1912 to 1926. (The occultist Madame

Blavatsky was a co-founder.) The society built more than a dozen structures on Temple Hill, many in a Moorish design known as "Islamic Egyptian," featuring onion-shaped roofs, softly arched doorways, keyhole windows, and other signature architectural features.

As you climb Temple Hill, you can see a large former Krotona building across the trees to your right. This is Moorcrest, once the society's finest private residence, and later home to, again, Charlie Chaplin. Nearer to hand, you'll find another Krotona residence at 6205—now an apartment building.

Follow Temple Hill as it crests and winds down, eventually crossing in front of Moorcrest. (The Batchelder tiles on its walls and the stars on its driveway gate are typical Theosophist details.) Bear right, and continue to the stop sign. Turn left, continuing along Temple Hill, pausing to notice the Krotona features on the building at 6108, and again across the street at 6107. At the corner, turn right onto N. Gower Street. At the next corner, turn right again onto Scenic Avenue. Turn left onto Vista Del Mar, rise up a block, and stop at the corner of Primrose.

Directly to your left are the ruins of a stone wall that once held a statue of the Blessed Virgin Mary. A wayward automobile took that out a few years ago. Now the tile remnants of the shrine are themselves a shrine, and usually contain a handful of votive candles.

Just across the street is Krotona itself. This large, shaded apartment building, still wearing the Krotona name, was home after its Theosophical Society days to another legendary Eastern spiritual leader—the charismatic Jiddu Krishnamurti. (His pen name, altered slightly for the street you walked earlier, was "Alcyone.") Inside the Krotona building are koi ponds, shady nooks, and extensive gardens.

Continue down Vista Del Mar. At the first corner, turn right into the alley-like Holly Mont Drive. The apartment building on your left, and the one up ahead of it, were both Theosophical Society/Krotona outbuildings at one time. Across the street, at 6215, is the former Barbara Stanwyck estate, known now as Hollymont Castle. Said to be haunted, it is currently the home of Dexter Grey, a virtuoso pianist and table tennis ace who has taken to decorating the classic Spanish Revival home with alarming statuary.

Grab the stairs going down across from Hollymont Castle. This is a beautiful double-barreled set of 61 steps, centered around a dry pond and shaded by a spreading palm, that drops you back down to Vista Del Mar. Walk down straight ahead, enjoying on the right side a set of recently renovated 1919 Mission Revival bungalows, at 2005. Continue down to Franklin, and return to your starting point.

If you are in the mood for something traditional after all the exotic spiritualism, go east one block to Gower, and north one block to Carmen Place, and visit the Monastery of the Angels. The sisters at this cloistered Dominican nunnery support themselves, in part, by baking and selling pumpkin bread and chocolates. Pumpkin loaves cost $9, and are on sale in the gift shop every day (except for Sunday) from 8:30 AM to 5:00 PM (except for a lunch hour at noon). It's a little steep for pumpkin bread, but after the long walk, you deserve the best.

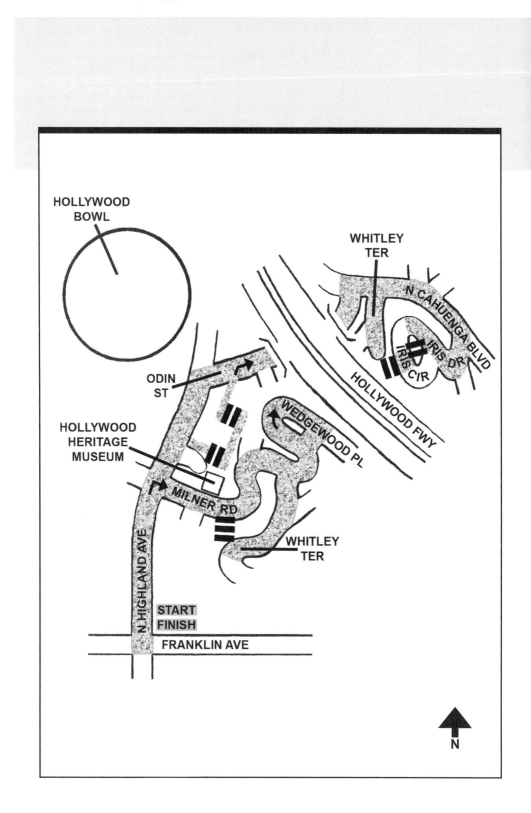

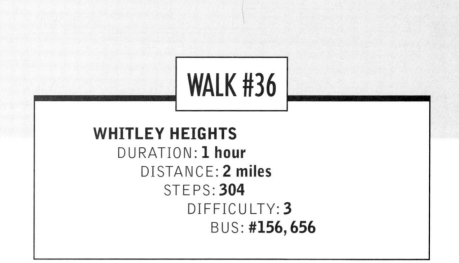

WALK #36

WHITLEY HEIGHTS
DURATION: **1 hour**
DISTANCE: **2 miles**
STEPS: **304**
DIFFICULTY: **3**
BUS: **#156, 656**

This is a gentle walk along some of Hollywood's oldest and most beautiful hillside streets, filled with stars' homes from filmdom's Golden Age, and hidden staircases and walkways.

Begin your walk near the intersection of Franklin Avenue and N. Highland Avenue, perhaps with a coffee from the Starbucks at the mini-mall on the corner. Walk north on Highland, on the east side of the street, heading toward the Hollywood Bowl. On the right you'll see the historic Highland Towers apartment building, said to have been William Faulkner's home while he worked on such films as *The Big Sleep* and *To Have and Have Not*. Across the street, check out the fine-looking Moorish building that houses American Legion Post 43.

At the corner, turn right onto Milner Road, ignoring the Hollywood Heritage Museum on your left for now. Instead, walk straight up Milner. Just past the house at 6676, you'll find your first staircase. These are the Whitley Terrace steps, one of the few sets in the city to have its own signpost. They're a beauty, too—a well-maintained, double-L-shaped construction of 160 steps. Halfway up, at about step 90, there are excellent views of

the High Tower residential area, featured in this book in Walk
#37. But since these steps walk right through people's front and
backyards, don't ooh and aah too much. Walk quietly and don't
make a fuss.

At the top of the stairs, landing at 6670 Whitley Terrace,
turn left and follow the road to where it merges with Grace Avenue, appreciating the fine old homes on both sides of the street,
like the two imposing Spanish structures at 6711 and 6717. Stay
on the left or downhill side, past the turning for Milner, and turn
left onto Wedgewood Place. Follow this around in a loop, pausing at 6758 to mourn the loss of a staircase. The public stairway going down to Fairfield Avenue, formerly a fine shortcut to
the Hollywood Bowl, has been gated and locked. Further along,
pause even longer to mourn the loss of Villa Valentino, home of
the silent film star Rudolph Valentino, 6776. It was removed in
the late 1940s to make room for the Hollywood Freeway, which
provides the roar you hear from the other side of the sound
wall standing where Villa Valentino once stood. Complete the
Wedgewood circle, and when you meet Milner again bear right
and head downhill.

If you have a taste for Hollywood history, take the turning to the right onto Watsonia Terrace. On this short block are
houses once owned or occupied by the famous costume designer Adrian (he did the ruby red slippers for *The Wizard of Oz*,
among other iconic items), W.C. Fields (whose home featured
a marble swimming pool), Gloria Swanson and, again, William
Faulkner.

Otherwise, stay to the left, on Milner. At 6758 you'll see
the remnants of an old public staircase that now rises straight up
into someone's backyard. (Its gate matches the one at the bottom of the Whitley Terrace staircase you climbed a while ago.)
Continue down past the Whitley Terrace steps, and turn right at
Highland into the Hollywood Heritage Museum parking lot. Off
to your right you'll see a flight of lovely old stairs leading up into
the trees. Take these, saving your tour of the museum for another day, up 59 steps into a picnic area. Follow the roadway to your

left, winding down to another set of steps going down on the right. Take these 13—half of them wooden—down to the parking lot, and continue to the right. At the end of the parking lot, you'll come to Odin Street. Turn right, and follow this past the turning for Fairfield and pass under the Hollywood Freeway.

The big boulevard in front of you is N. Cahuenga Boulevard. (Above, you can see a big white cross, erected to honor Christine Wetherill Stevenson, founder of a religious playhouse originally known as the Pilgrimage Theater. It was built in 1920, burned down shortly after Stevenson's death two years later, then rebuilt, taken over by the county, and named after county supervisor John Anson Ford, whose name it bears today.) Turn right, and then turn right immediately after, back onto another section of Whitley Terrace—the other side of the street now divided by the freeway. Follow this up to the very end. At the far left corner, you'll find a hidden staircase that will carry you 27 steps up onto Iris Circle. Turn right.

Keeping a sharp eye out, just after the house at 6808, find the 16 steps up onto the very secluded walkway that bisects this curious little street. Follow this deeply shaded, almost overgrown sidewalk back to the other side of Iris Circle. Turn right.

At 6860, you'll see one of the city's most charming staircases—a faux-wooden construction of steps and rails, made of concrete, surrounding a fine-looking fishpond. Unfortunately, this is not a public staircase. You could take the steps down to Cahuenga, but it would be wrong. Instead, take Iris downhill to the corner, turn left, and then turn left onto Cahuenga again. Follow this back to Odin, turn left, and make another left again into the Hollywood Heritage Museum parking lot. Highland will take you back to your starting point.

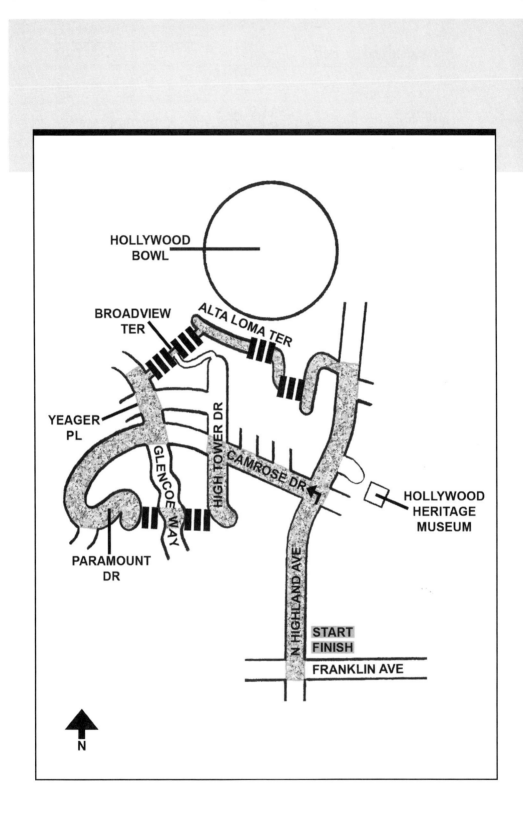

HOLLYWOOD BOWL AND HIGH TOWER LOOP
DURATION: **1 hour, 30 minutes**
DISTANCE: **2.6 miles**
STEPS: **421**
DIFFICULTY: **4**
BUS: **#156, 656**

This is an exotic stairwalk around the back side of the Hollywood Bowl, into one of the city's few walk-street communities, with no access to cars. It's heavy on history, dotted with architectural gems, and full of atmosphere.

Park your car somewhere near the intersection of Franklin and Highland Avenues. There's a Starbucks on the corner, in the mini-mall. Get a coffee, and go.

Walk directly north on Highland Avenue, passing the fine old Highland Towers apartment building, where William Faulkner is said to have lived while writing the screenplay for the adaptations of Ernest Hemingway's *To Have and Have Not* and Raymond Chandler's *The Big Sleep*. Farther up the block, you may admire the Moorish American Legion building across the way.

At the corner of Milner Avenue, cross Highland to the opposite side and begin walking uphill on Camrose Drive. Go past Woodland Way, and Rockledge Road. Take the first left, onto High Tower Drive.

Don't spoil the fun for yourself: don't turn around and look behind. Instead, walk straight on to the cul-de-sac end of the block, and find the first set of stairs. These are clean, well swept, and abut an enormous garden of eucalyptus trees behind chain-link fence and barbed wire.

The first stage rises across eight landings and up 103 steps—I could find no contractor's name or date, but the inspector's stamp said "H. Harken"—and drops you on the flat, poorly paved cul-de-sac end of Glencoe Way.

Turn to your right, now, and across valley you can see and really appreciate the view of High Tower itself. Looking like an Italian campanile, it is actually an elevator shaft built in the 1920s. Much more about this later.

(Should you want to extend your walk, turn left and head south on Glencoe. Slow to admire the drum kit sculpture on your right, then continue toward the Mediterranean-style complex just ahead. Follow the walkway—it's a public pathway, though it looks private—and find the continuation of Glencoe on the other side. Where the road bends, you will find the Samuel Freeman House, a Frank Lloyd Wright textile block construction from 1924 (the same period as Wright's Ennis and Hollyhock houses), now owned by the University of Southern California. When you've enjoyed this, retrace your steps, and return to Glencoe.)

For now, cross Glencoe to the next set of stairs, and keep climbing over a challenging 110 steps. There is a handrail for the first section, and none after.

At the top, another flat section of another cul-de-sac, is Paramount Drive. Turn right, and follow Paramount down and to the right as it turns back into Camrose and heads downhill. Walk to the first corner and turn left on Glencoe. Walk to the first corner and turn left on Glencoe. Walk one short block, and turn right onto Yeager Place. Just to your left you'll see the bottom of Broadview Terrace. This short alley-like street will shortly become a staircase, and your gateway into High Tower.

This architectural oddity has appeared in many iconic Los Angeles novels, as characters like Raymond Chandler's Philip Marlowe and Michael Connelly's Harry Bosch have trod past it looking for suspects. The campanile-style tower was built by developer Carl Kay in the 1920s to serve the Alta Loma community of homeowners. Only 30 residents, it is said, have keys to this exclusive conveyance.

If you're not one of them, walk up the 23 steps that form the first section of the Broadview steps, until the walkway meets the Los Altos Place steps. (This is a rare occurrence in Los Angeles—the intersection of two walk-streets.) Climb the next flight of 37 steps to a pathway that offers a better view of the High Tower elevator and of downtown Hollywood. Continue, and climb 52 more steps, to the large Streamline Moderne-style white home on your left. You're in Alta Loma.

The home at 2200 Broadview was designed by Lloyd Wright, son of Frank Lloyd. Appreciate that, then turn right down the narrow concrete pathway, and enter the strange, serene, private world of Alta Loma. It's a honeycomb of thin passages, wooden fences, and lush gardens obscuring most of the architecture. The bougainvillea and trumpet vines are thick, and the air is full of silence, shade and, some mornings, the smell of someone baking pastries.

Alta Loma Terrace eases downhill, sloping past a Japanese-themed estate on the right and an ancient clapboard boarding house on the left. The walkway is tidy and well kept, and the hillside is so thick with foliage that you can entirely forget how near you are to the civilization you've left behind—until you catch glimpses of the Hollywood Bowl parking lot, between the houses, a hundred feet over to your left.

At the bottom of the sloping walkway, the path drops down 18 steps and turns right, drops another four. Note the charming old "Alta Loma" sign on the corner. Then take the hard left as the walkway continues down, over an elegant collection of four matched sets of 14 steps and a final 10. You will land in a parking lot. Turn left, and go past the garages cut into the side of the hill. At the far end of the parking lot, to the right, you'll find a large black swing gate—locked against entry, but allowing exit—that will deposit you back on Highland Ave. Turn right, down Highland, to your starting point.

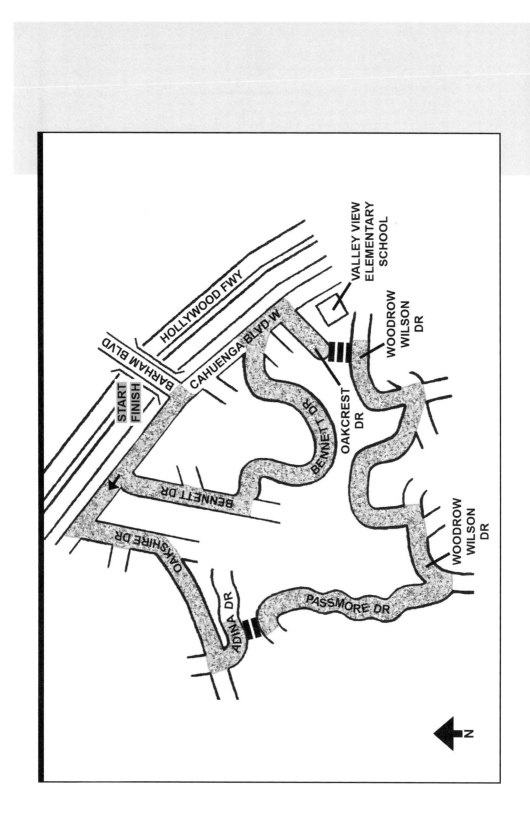

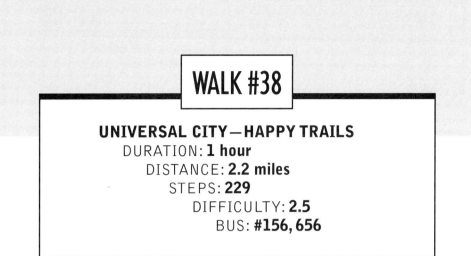

WALK #38

UNIVERSAL CITY—HAPPY TRAILS
DURATION: **1 hour**
DISTANCE: **2.2 miles**
STEPS: **229**
DIFFICULTY: **2.5**
BUS: **#156, 656**

This is a curious hillside walk, in the shadow of Mulholland Drive, which overlooks Universal Studios and the San Fernando Valley. It features two staircases, some architectural wonders, and a network of paved, interlacing "trails."

Begin your walk near the intersection of Cahuenga Boulevard West and Barham Boulevard, perhaps with a coffee from the Starbucks just north of that corner. Cross to the west side of Cahuenga—away from the Hollywood Freeway and Universal Studios—and begin walking north, or downhill. Pass Bennett Drive, and then turn left at the next signal, onto Oakshire Drive.

The road becomes quieter and greener, with huge eucalyptus and sycamore trees. Walk past cozy houses with tidy yards, bearing right where Oakshire meets Ellington Drive. Stay on Oakshire, as the houses get bigger. Make the hard left onto Adina Drive, and begin walking uphill.

The road gets steeper, and the shade gets deeper. Adina rises and crests and, just as it begins to fall again, presents its first staircase, one house after the big white rectangle at 3343.

This is a fine-looking structure, fitted with double metal handrails at the bottom and some wobbly wooden rails the rest of the way. It's unswept and a little messy, but free of trash and graffiti. Walk up 146 steps, over several landings, under good shade, to land at 3012 Passmore Drive.

Turn left, under a huge oak tree, and begin walking uphill. As you go, getting views of Griffith Park and the Hollywood sign, the houses become grander and more absurd. Enjoy "Wings," the Flintstones-meets-Jetsons structure at 2955.

Continue on up as Passmore winds around the side of the impressive La Soledad at 2942, with its cheery "Surviving Trespassers Will Be Prosecuted" sign. The canyon below is the high end of Ellington, the turn you didn't take earlier, which ends in a gated private community of several houses.

At the turning, where Passmore meets Woodrow Wilson Drive, turn left, pausing to admire the brick-and-shingle job at 7270, with its many elaborate terraces and, depending on your language skills, the message carved into the lintel over the garage. It reads, "Huset Karl Har Bygget Dorthea." My best Norwegian translates this as "House Charles (or Karl) Has Built Dorthea (or Dorothy.)"

Head left down Woodrow Wilson, enjoying wide views of Universal City and Universal Studios. Walk along, under broad oaks and sycamores, avoiding the turnings for the first of the area's many paved "trails." First up is Valevista Trail. Next is Sycamore Trail. (Nearby are Goodview, Sunnydell, Viso, and Vanland Trail, as well as the odd-sounding Woody, Packwood, and Treasure Trail.)

The views improve as you wind along, bringing you horizons of the San Fernando Valley and, off to the far left, another look at "Wings" and its long railroad-tie hillside staircase.

Coming along at 7149, you'll see the first of a series of cantilevered hillside homes that might remind you of the traditional Batak houses of Indonesia—long, boat-like structures common to Sumatra and the other islands of that archipelago. It also might remind you, if you're literary, of scenes from mystery novelist Michael Connelly, whose serial hero Harry Bosch lives in one of these homes.

You'll get better views as you wind around the hillside of the Batak houses. But reserve your real excitement for the house on your right, just before the intersection where Woodrow Wilson meets Pacific View Drive. This mosaic-tiled 1927 masterpiece, with its domes, minarets, and arched windows, represents the life work of George Ehling, a professional wrestler *cum* actor *cum* tile artist. (That's his family motto—"Alla Buona in La Famiglia Ehling"—over one door, and his self-portrait in stone over another.) Almost every inch of the 4,700-square-foot home is dotted with intricate mosaic and it's a wonder to behold.

Turn left, staying on Woodrow Wilson as it meets Pacific View. Wind down and around, past Loyal Trail, getting another look at the side of the Hollywood sign and a peek at the Griffith Observatory. After the house at 7001 on the left, find your final set of stairs.

This is another nicely-designed staircase, with metal railings, deeply shaded but not very well maintained, that drops 83 steps down to land at the cul-de-sac end of Oakcrest Drive. Walk straight ahead, down quite a steep stretch of city street, as the road slides past Valley View Elementary School—for whose students' benefit, probably, that last staircase was constructed. At the bottom of the hill, turn left onto Cahuenga. Walk past Fire Station No. 76, and past the turning for Cadet Court, but then veer left and up the hill onto Bennett Drive.

This is a quiet stretch of street, green with trees, offering a little respite from the noise of Cahuenga and the Hollywood Freeway. There's a nice tiled fountain at 3236, and a rare Hachiya persimmon tree a little farther along on the left. Later, you come to a turning for Carse Drive, which makes a loop up into that box canyon and meets Ellington—but is private and off-limits to everyday citizens. Continue on Bennett as it curves around, begins to flatten and drop, and ultimately deposits you back on Cahuenga—across the street from Starbucks, near your original starting point.

PART FIVE

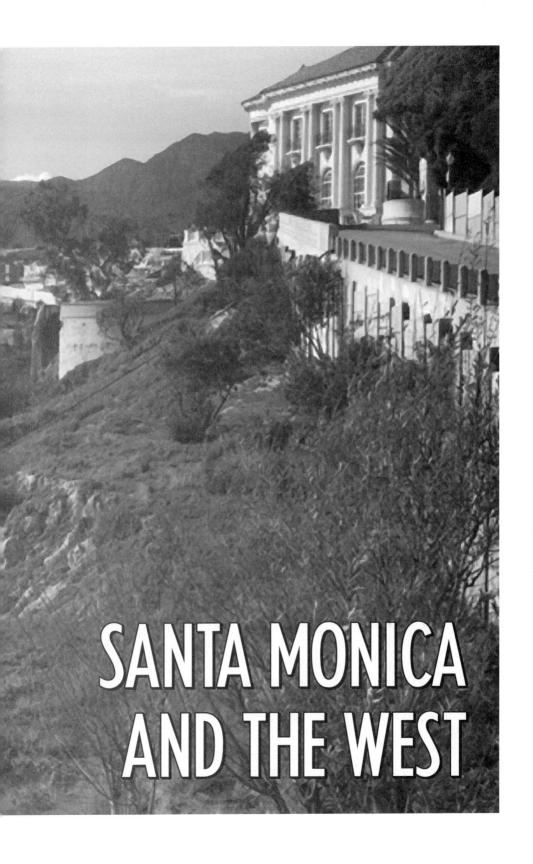

SANTA MONICA
AND THE WEST

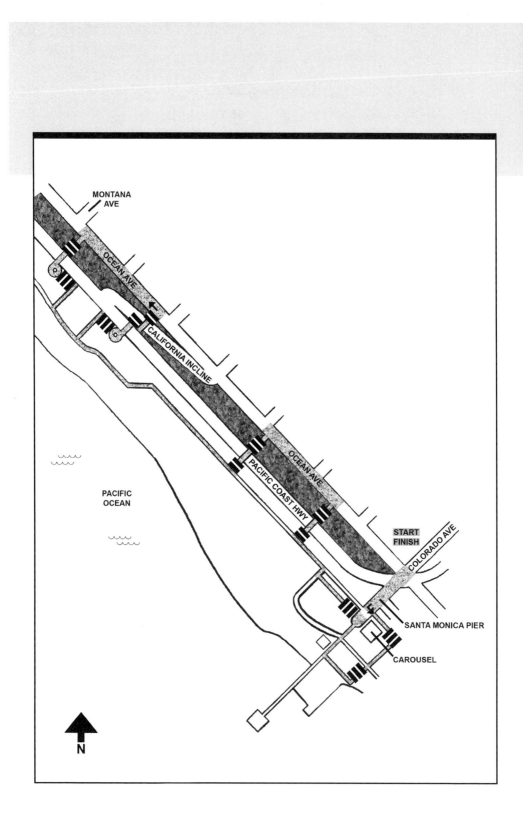

MONTANA AVE

OCEAN AVE

CALIFORNIA INCLINE

OCEAN AVE

PACIFIC COAST HWY

PACIFIC OCEAN

START FINISH

COLORADO AVE

SANTA MONICA PIER

CAROUSEL

N

SANTA MONICA—BLUFFS AND BEACH WALK
DURATION: **1 hour, 30 minutes**
DISTANCE: **3.5 miles**
STEPS: **384 to 450**
DIFFICULTY: **3**
BUS: **#20, 534; Santa Monica
Bus #1, 7**

This is a great combination walk—big stairs, huge Pacific views, and long stretches of flat pathway filled with interesting historical bits. It can be very hot in summer and somewhat windy in winter, but the vistas are sensational.

Begin your walk near the top of the Santa Monica Pier, near the intersection of Ocean Avenue and Colorado Avenue, perhaps after lunch or coffee at Il Fornaio, or an excellent seafood meal at The Lobster, or an inexpensive coffee and donut on the pier. In any case, start by walking onto the pier and heading out over the water.

Down the ramp, on your left, is the historic merry-go-round. It was built in 1915 and is one of the world's last wooden carousels, and may look familiar: It co-starred with Paul Newman and Robert Redford in the 1973 film *The Sting*. (It's where Newman was working and hanging out at the beginning of the movie.) The pier itself dates from 1909, and used to feature a "Blue Streak Racer" rollercoaster and the La Monica Ballroom, a 15,000-square-foot dance hall.

Turn left off the ramp just in front of the carousel, and

cross the boardwalk, keeping the carousel on your right. Head for a flight of wooden stairs going down through a clump of palm trees, and drop nine steps down, and then nine steps more, to the street level. You can get a snack here, and even assault your stomach with a Hot Dog on a Stick. Turn right in front of the volleyball courts and follow the path toward the water, keeping the pier on your right. Cross the bicycle path—carefully, since they have the right of way and *will* run you down—and take the 26 steps back up to the pier level. Cross the parking lot, heading for the Bubba Gump Shrimp Co. sign, then turn right and head up the pier's main street. Just in front of the carousel, you'll find another set of stairs, dropping down 19 paces on the left. Take these back to street level, and begin walking north on the beach pedestrian path ahead of you.

The parking lot on your right was once the site of the Deauville Beach Club, a massive, pyramid-topped leisure center built in 1927 and destroyed by fire in 1955. (It was one of many—Casa Del Mar, Sorrento, Edgewater, and Miramar among them—that dominated beach life in the 1930s and 1940s. Today, only The Jonathan Club and The Beach Club still remain.) At the end of the parking lot, head for the pedestrian overpass on your right. Take the 42 sloping stairs up to the curved walkway, cross Pacific Coast Highway, then climb the winding construction of 44 brick stairs to the Santa Monica bluffs.

At the top, you'll land on Ocean Ave. across from The Georgian Hotel, an Art Deco delight from 1933. Nearer to hand is an old cannon, reportedly an 1861 naval artillery piece. Walk north, past the cannon, and begin enjoying Santa Monica's Palisades Park. The views here are sublime and stretch from Malibu to Catalina and beyond, with the Santa Monica Mountains presiding. There are benches if you want to stop and rest to look at the *faux bois* concrete handrails dating from the turn of the century—the *last* century, the 1900s—and an interesting collection of vagrants, homeless people, senior citizens, and tourists soaking up the sunshine, as well as a steady stream of joggers and cyclists. It makes for excellent people watching. You can also amuse yourself by searching for the famous crisscross "W" palm trees that marked the site of buried treasure in the 1963 film *It's a Mad Mad Mad Mad World*, or the top of the legendary "99 Steps" staircase, built in 1875, that took sunbathers down to the sand back when there was nothing down there *but* sand.

Continue north along the bluffs. Just past the memorial to the armed forces on your left, parallel to the intersection with Arizona Avenue on your right, find the next set of stairs heading down. These date from 1935—when they replaced the original wooden "99 Steps"—and will carry you 70 steps down onto a pedestrian overpass crossing the PCH again, and another 36 steps down to pavement level. Turn right, along PCH, then turn left immediately into the parking lot, and walk to the pedestrian pathway running along the beach. Continue north.

Here you will find one of the several Perry's Beach Café locations, where you can get a snack or a soda, or rent a bicycle or a set of roller blades. Follow the pedestrian pathway north along the parking lot. Where the bike path veers to the left and toward the ocean, follow it—being mindful that it is a bike path, where two-wheelers have the right of way. Walk toward the clump of palm trees in the sand, past The Jonathan Club and several small public parking lots, until you come to the bright umbrellas that mark another Perry's Beach Café. Turn here into parking lot #7, cross the lot, and head for the sweeping circular walkway leading to your next staircase—up the ramp, over the highway onto the California Incline, up a set of 32 stairs to a walkway over the Incline, and up a final ramp and a final 16 steps.

Back on top of the bluffs, head left and continue walking north beneath the palms. You'll note public restrooms here, and other curiosities, including a shopping cart dispensing area. The City of Santa Monica knows that homeless people need shopping carts, so they supply them, and the parking spaces they go into when they're no longer needed.

Nearing Montana Avenue, the parkway narrows to a single sidewalk, and then broadens again. Just here, look for the next staircase, falling down to your left. This is a noble old wooden structure, likely to be muddy on wet days, that drops 133 steps over multiple landings, connects to a walkway going over the PCH once more, and culminates in an elegant circular stairway with 34 steps down to the beach level.

There are tiles in the sidewalk here that read "The Gables." They are all that remains, except for some remnants of wall across the PCH, of Santa Monica's first and grandest beach club. It was a massive structure, built in the early 1920s, with a gable-windowed beach house on the sand and a 10-story French chateau-style building rising from the PCH to the top of the bluffs. It was destroyed by fire not long after its construction.

Cross the parking lot, taking the pedestrian path to the right of the public restrooms, and rejoin the bike path. To the right, heading north, your options include the Back On the Beach Café—the only restaurant in the area where you can actually sit on the beach, with your toes in the sand, and eat a meal—or the newly opened Annenberg Community Beach House. The magnificent 110-room mansion was built in the late 1920s by newspaper magnate William Randolph Hearst for his mistress Marion Davies, with designs by architect Julia Morgan, who did Hearst Castle in San Simeon and Hearst's Herald Examiner building in Downtown Los Angeles. The property was later operated as the Oceanhouse Hotel, and later still as The Sand & Sea Club. It is now run by the city of Santa Monica—thanks to substantial funding from the Annenberg family—and is open to the public.

To your left, heading south, turn back toward the pier. For additional exercise, you may take any one of the pedestrian crossings back up the stairs to the bluffs, and continue south to the head of the pier, or walk along the bike path and to the pier itself. Either way, you will complete your loop and return to your starting point.

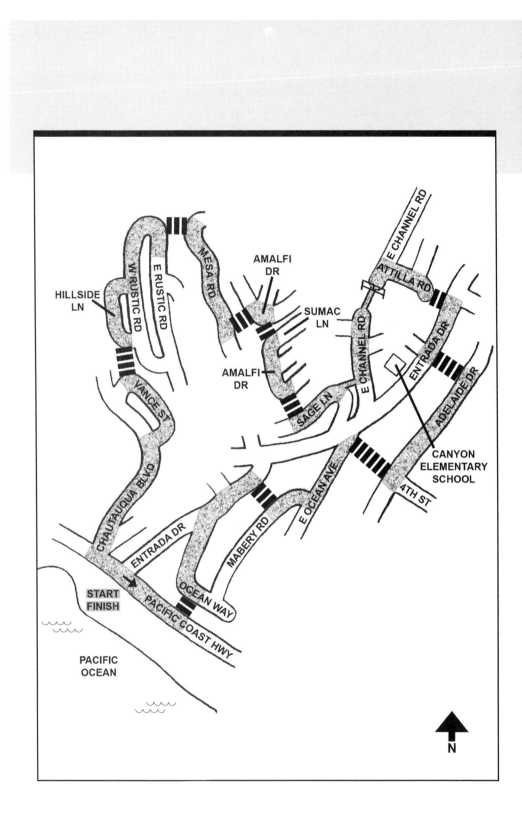

SANTA MONICA — RUSTIC CANYON LOOP
DURATION: **1 hour, 45 minutes**
DISTANCE: **3 miles**
STEPS: **1,069**
DIFFICULTY: **4.5**
BUS: **#534; Santa Monica Bus #9**

This is an athletic walk up the southern side of Santa Monica Canyon and back down into bucolic Rustic Canyon, through leafy, eucalyptus-scented glades and past historic homes and architectural wonders. Along the way are hard bodies and ocean views.

Start your walk in Santa Monica Canyon, near the intersection of Entrada Drive and Pacific Coast Highway. You may consider breakfast at Patrick's Roadhouse, once the favored eatery of local strongmen like Bruce Willis and Arnold Schwarzenegger, for fueling up.

Leaving there, walk south on PCH, past the gas station, to the first staircase. It rises to the left, 48 steps up to Ocean Way. Head left, down the hill, to where Ocean merges with Entrada Dr., and continue to 278 Entrada. There, find the second stairway, a shady green corridor that rises 169 steps up to Mabery Rd. Turn left, and follow Mabery to its intersection with East Ocean Avenue. Cross the street, carefully.

You will see a set of stairs just up the hill. Don't be fooled. This is a remnant of an old staircase that ran along the side of

Ocean and connected it, ultimately, to the westernmost block of Adelaide Drive. If you follow it now, you will wind up at the back door of an apartment building with no access to Adelaide, or anything else.

Instead, turn left down Ocean. At the corner, turn right, and witness the wonder of the famous 4th Street steps.

On any given weekend day, this is more of an outside gymnasium than a public staircase. Some of the fittest folks you'll ever see treat this as their own private outdoor Stairmaster. (And some enterprising person has installed a soft-drink vending machine at the bottom of the steps, well hidden on your right.) But be aware that while you are walking, the hard bodies are working out. You are in their way. They will grumble if you aren't going fast enough. So stay in single file (if you're walking in a group), and keep to the right.

The staircase is a grueling 189 steps over multiple stages, up an extremely steep hillside. (Inch for inch, it may be the steepest staircase in the city, which may be why it is equipped with handrails on both sides.) At the top, as you catch your breath, turn left and head up Adelaide.

There are splendid views here of the ocean and the facing Rustic Canyon hillside. There are also marvelous homes, including a very fine Craftsman on the corner, built in 1905 by Elmer Hunt and Myron Grey—who also did the famous Wattles residence in Hollywood. At 145 Adelaide is the former home of British novelist Christopher Isherwood, who in 1952 called Santa Monica Canyon "our western Greenwich Village." Farther east, you can see Robert Stacy-Judd's remarkable Zuni House at 710 Adelaide. Further west, at 142, is the Henry Weaver House, built in 1910 from a design by the architects responsible for Chinese and Egyptian Theaters in Hollywood.

What you should *not* see is anyone stretching or exercising on the 4th St. grass median; local homeowners were so irritated by the stair-climbers using their street as an exercise studio that they've called upon police to issue tickets to anyone doing push-ups or sit-ups on the grass. I have been told the stairs would have been closed to the public altogether, but for one peculiar fact: They *can't* be, because they are part of the region's tsunami escape system, and must be kept open in the event of such an emergency.

Heading east on Adelaide, away from the ocean, enjoy the canyon views off to the left and look for the next staircase midway up the next block. This is a fine old set of 166 wooden steps. Halfway down, they cross a driveway—the only public staircase in the city, I think, that is interrupted by a private drive. At the bottom, you'll find more evidence of hard bodies at work—discarded bottles of Evian and other workout detritus.

Cross Entrada carefully here—there is no crosswalk—and turn right. Walk uphill a few hundred feet, and find the next staircase on your left. This is a short set of 25 stairs that land on the cul-de-sac end of Attilla Road. Walk straight ahead on Attilla, and then turn left at the first opportunity onto East Channel Road. A block on, East Channel will end at a wide metal gate. Walk past the gate, down the alley, until you meet East Channel's other side. Continue, with Canyon Elementary School on your left, until you find a crosswalk and a pedestrian bridge crossing the creek on your right. Take the bridge, and walk straight ahead, onto Sage Lane.

At the end of this little street, you will find a staircase on the right. Take it, rising up one set of 14 steps and, turning to the right, another set of 64 steps to the top.

Now you're on Amalfi Drive. Walk straight from the top of the stairs until Amalfi turns right. Go straight, onto Sumac Lane. At the elbow where Sumac begins to bend to the right, find your next staircase on the left, at 323 Sumac. It's another steep one, affording fine shade on a hot day, that runs narrowly between two large houses—124 steps, straight up, with very few breaks.

Take a breather. You're on Amalfi again, but not for long. Walk the width of just one house and look to the left. You'll find a staircase that looks private but isn't. Take the 124 stairs down, carefully—there is no handrail here, and the steps are steep.

At the bottom, you're now on Mesa Road. Take this up to the right, and just past the delightful Streamline Moderne house at 475 Mesa. This is the Entenza House, built in 1937 by Harwell Hamilton Harris for John Entenza, then the editor of *Arts & Architecture* magazine. (Entenza had a more famous house built some years later by Ray and Charles Eames and Eero Saarinen. It's the Case Study House #9, and is near the end of this walk, at 205 Chautauqua Boulevard.)

If you were to continue up Mesa a block or so, and turn left, you'd enter the section of Rustic Canyon once known as Uplifters Ranch. This was the name given to a private drinking club, established during Prohibition, on property owned by the cowboy celebrity Will Rogers. He and his pals played polo on a field further up the canyon. They held high-powered parties at Uplifters until Prohibition ended, then sold the property off as individual home sites.

For now though, enjoy the circular Entenza carport, and catch the staircase just past it on the left, at 491 Mesa. It has a sign that says "Pedestrians Use Caution." It's a silly warning—who else is going to be on that staircase, except pedestrians?—but useful: These 61 steps are steep and uneven, and don't offer a good handrail. Watch your step, and land at 550 East Rustic Road.

At the bottom of the steps, walk straight ahead to East Rustic Road, turn right, and make the bend onto West Rustic Road. Go along to the first corner, and turn right onto Hillside Lane. Follow that to the next corner, where on the right side, at 419 Hillside, you will find the day's final staircase. Again, this is a deeply shaded, narrow walkway that looks very much like a private staircase, but isn't. Take the 85 stairs up to Vance Street.

Follow Vance downhill along an odd, unpaved section of road, past the eccentric Spanish tile work at the house on your left, until the pavement starts again and meets Chautauqua Blvd. Turn left, taking great care to stay on the sidewalk of this busy street as you drop down the hill. You'll find yourself at the intersection of West Channel Rd. and the PCH. Cross the street and go south along the highway, back to your starting point.

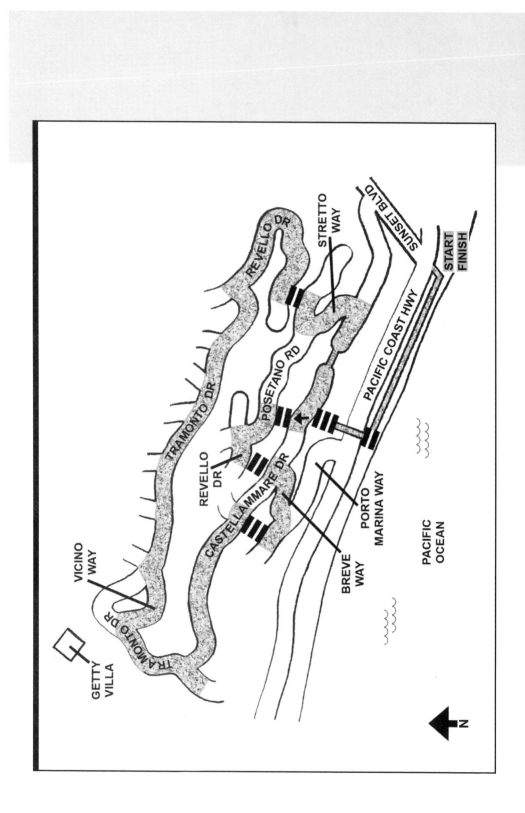

PACIFIC PALISADES—CASTELLAMMARE
DURATION: **1 hour, 15 minutes**
DISTANCE: **3.2 miles**
STEPS: **518**
DIFFICULTY: **3.5**
BUS: **#2, 302, 430**

The most scenic of all the city's stairwalks, this hillside stroll offers sweeping Pacific views, ocean breezes, and grisly Hollywood film lore. Its handsome hidden staircases are adjacent to the Getty Villa, the Self-Realization Fellowship, and Topanga Park, making it an ideal all-day recreation destination.

Find yourself by bus or car at the doorstep of Gladstone's of Malibu, the popular seaside seafood restaurant at the corner of Sunset Boulevard and Pacific Coast Highway. You may enjoy a few sunny moments on their patio, whether you are a customer or not—the patio is public property. You may picnic here, and even bring your own food, as long as you first request a table from the host station at the Gladstone's entrance. The restrooms here, and coastal access, are also open to the public, though the parking is not. (There is, however, a warning: Across the street, on Sunset, is a sign saying, "Entering Tsunami Hazard Area." What you're meant to *do* with this information, I don't know, but there are similar signs in Santa Monica Canyon and as far south as Laguna Beach, and as far north as Humboldt County. The community of Port Hueneme, in Ventura County, has a tsunami warning *siren*.)

Begin walking north, on the ocean side of PCH, through the parking lot behind Gladstone's. You'll notice remnants of old staircases and an old promenade on the eastern side of the highway—wiped out not by tidal waves, but by the landslides that have plagued the area. Continue past a bank of public restrooms (fitted with outdoor showers), and past lifeguard tower #2 to the pedestrian overpass crossing PCH. Take the stairs up and over—35 steps up, a walkway across the highway, then 40 steps up again—to land on Castellammare Drive.

The big, white Spanish structure you've just walked over was once known as Thelma Todd's Sidewalk Café, a roadhouse-speakeasy operated by the film actress of that name. Ms. Todd, who died nearby under suspicious circumstances in 1935, was the blonde beauty featured in the Marx Brothers' *Monkey Business* and *Horsefeathers*. She was found dead in her Lincoln Phaeton, killed by carbon monoxide poisoning. Suspects in the case included her boyfriend, her business partner, her ex-husband, and the gangster Lucky Luciano. The building now houses the inspirational film company Paulist Productions.

Cross Castellammare and walk a short few steps uphill to the next staircase, a steep construction with green handrails, rising 69 steps and lifting you to Posetano Road. Across the street, behind a wooden barricade, you will see evidence that the steps used to continue on up the hill. A series of landslides wiped out that staircase, and several others, and closed pieces of roadway all over the Castellammare hillside. You can still see some staircase wreckage rising behind the barricade.

So, turn left onto Posetano and walk to the next corner. Here, another stair remnant. There is a lovely flight of finely maintained stairs rising straight up from the intersection. These stairs end on a platform, and serve nothing—except to deliver a better view of the sunset, perhaps. Turn left down Revello Drive instead, and just after the house at 17712, find the nearly hidden staircase going down on the left.

Like most of the staircases in the Castellammare area,

this set is marked with a contractor's stamp reading "Braun, Bryant + Austin," and is dated 1927. This one is two flights, 91 steps total, and quite steep, but fitted with handrails. It deposits you at the corner of Breve Way and Castellammare. Follow Breve down to the right, to where it meets Porto Marina Way. Across the road, you can see the remnants of yet another fine old staircase. This one is broad and beautifully built, and delivers you more or less into the traffic on PCH.

You don't want that. Instead, climb Porto Marina to just past the house at 17737, and find your next staircase. This one, another Braun, Bryant + Austin, rises 86 steps and drops you back on Castellammare. Turn left, and continue uphill. High above on your right, you may see the pilings supporting the enormous villa at 17800 Tramonto Drive, and above them, a cantilevered tennis court and gravity-defying patio. Enormous efforts have been made to hold the hillside together here, including, at street level, sheets of raw iron that look like a Richard Serra construction.

Past this, and just past the house at 17878, hidden in bougainvillea in the vacant lot below, you can see the remnants of yet another abandoned staircase. This one is still in good working order, though it is entirely overrun. It drops down through some underbrush, and past the concrete foundations of a ruined house, dropping down 61 steps to Porto Marina Way. There is an unlocked gate at the bottom and the stairs are open, but not recommended.

Instead, continue up Castellammare a little further, enjoying the ocean breezes and mountain views. At the first corner, turn left and walk downhill a bit. Here at the edge of the bluffs is Villa de Leon, the Italianate mansion designed in 1928 by architect Kenneth MacDonald for wool magnate Leon Kauffman. The 12,000-square-foot limestone residence features marble floors, a circular ocean-view dining room, nine bedrooms, 11 bathrooms, and a seven-car garage with its own car wash. Four naked wood nymphs watch over the road. Over the door is the head of a fierce looking ram, keeping an eye on the wool-bearing sheep that made the Kauffman fortune.

Turn around and go back up the hill. You're on Tramon-to Drive now. Down and left, across the canyon, you will catch glimpses of the magnificent Getty Villa and surrounding glades and gardens. Continue uphill, then turn right onto Vicino Way. At the next corner, bear right back onto Tramonto. Though a contractor's stamp on the pavement sets the date of the street at 1927, most of the houses here are of more recent construc-tion. Pause at 17800, the 6,000-square-foot confection, built in 1931, whose cantilevered tennis court you admired from below.

Press on along Tramonto. Near the houses at 17646 and 17612 the Pacific spreads out before you. The ocean views are magnificent, and on the hillsides below you can see evidence of the landslides that put some of the now-defunct staircases out of business.

Down and around you go. Turn right at the T-intersec-tion where Tramonto meets Revello Drive, and follow Revello down until it crosses the narrow bridge and approaches its cul-de-sac end. But, just before that, you'll find another Braun, Bryant + Austin staircase on the left. It's a nicely balanced set of 122 steps, over four staircases, 25 steps each, bottomed out with a set of 22.

This will land you on Posetano Rd. once again. Turn right, go to the corner of Stretto Way, and stop. Here is Castillo Del Mar, a looming blue and brown structure that was the home of Thelma Todd at the time of her asphyxiated death. Take a deep breath, enjoy the sea air, and continue down Stretto. Where it meets Castellammare, turn right. Follow this down to the end of the road.

Castellammare used to continue, and return to its meet-ing with Breve and Porto Marina. But those landslides from the 1960s and '70s shut it down. Today, there's a nice little path go-ing where the road once led. Take this path, down one side and up the other. After you are back on pavement, just past the house 17560, find the final staircase to cross PCH once more.

For one final stairwalk thrill, walk down the last 14 steps

(more or less, depending on how much sand the tide has pushed onto the beach), take your shoes off and complete this walk along the shore. You can access the Gladstone's parking lot from the beach side, and you are back where you began.

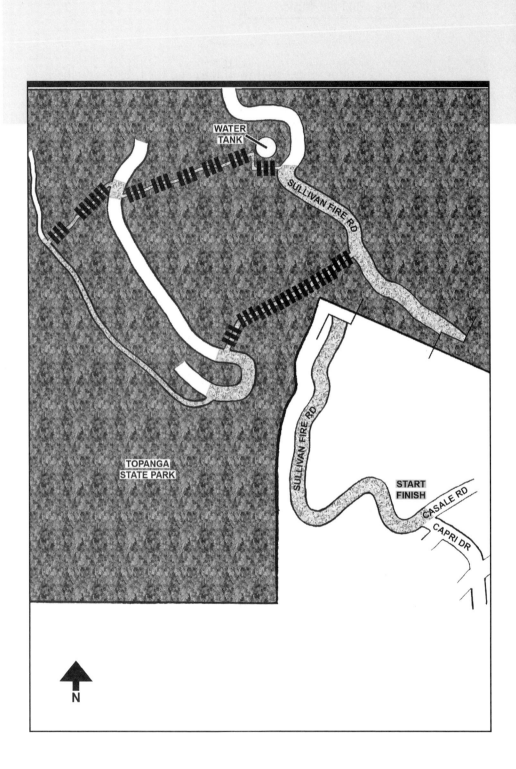

WALK #42

PACIFIC PALISADES—GIANT STEPS
DURATION: **1 hour, 30 minutes**
DISTANCE: **3.6 miles**
STEPS: **1,117**
DIFFICULTY: **5**
BUS: **#2, 302, 430**

Here is the monster step walk, a lovely, bucolic stroll through a secluded canyon that culminates in a hideous climb of over 500 steps, in a single staircase! Alone among the walks in this book, it is over stairs not originally intended for public use, on a route that offers no café or restaurant and no public restrooms, and is not well served by bus or Metro. But it is a walk of staggering beauty, over public parkland, filled with historical interest. Plus, it has that 500-step staircase!

Begin your walk high above the Pacific Palisades Riviera section, as far north of Sunset Boulevard as you can drive on Capri Drive. If it's a warm day, bring water—there's no café here. Stop and park at the corner of Capri and Casale Road and begin walking downhill on Casale. After a short distance, Casale becomes the Sullivan Fire Road. Walk straight ahead, past a derelict white structure on your left, until you come to a wide yellow fire gate. On the other side, as the signs tell you, you are entering Topanga State Park via the Rustic Canyon entrance. The signs also tell you to be alert for mountain lions. Walk straight ahead, anyway.

After 100 feet or so, you may note a set of wooden railroad-tie stairs going down into the canyon on your left. Ignore these, please. Ignore for now, too, the matching set of railroad-tie stairs rising up the canyon wall on the opposite side. These carry hikers up into Will Rogers State Park, and to the Backbone Trail that runs along the ridgeline ahead of you. Great hiking for another day. Today, continue straight on the paved road ahead of you.

Behind you, the views of Rustic Canyon, Santa Monica Canyon, the city of Santa Monica, and the Pacific Ocean will improve as you walk along, gaining altitude. You may also catch sight of another railroad-tie staircase heading down. Eventually, you will come to a pair of metal posts, and a trail that down below turns into a paved path. Ignore these, too, and press on.

When you have been walking for approximately 20–25 minutes, you will come to a chain-link fence, topped with barbed wire. This is the outer edge of the gigantic canyon estate built in the 1930s by Winona Stephens. According to local historians, Ms. Stephens, heir to a mining fortune, was persuaded by a man named Schmidt to invest $4 million in building a 50-acre, self-sustaining compound, complete with its own water and power system and capable of withstanding military assault. Lore has it Schmidt was a Nazi and believed Hitler's rising forces would one day take over America. Stephens funded construction of water tanks, diesel fuel tanks, and electric power generators, as well as living quarters for an army of Schmidt's followers. Frank Lloyd Wright was asked to submit a bid for additional construction. The compound functioned smoothly until the onset of World War II. Schmidt was identified as a Nazi spy, and arrested. He died in prison. Winona Stephens's hideaway fell into disrepair, and the land was subsequently deeded to the state.

About 120 feet from the start of the fence, there is a gate. Through this gate is a concrete staircase with a magnificent view of the surrounding mountains and the canyons and sea below. Stop and admire the view, but don't take the stairs. Return to the road, and continue downhill a bit. After only 100 feet or so, you will find a second gate and, a few feet inside it, another staircase. This is your first set of stairs. Begin walking downhill.

Down and to your right is one of the remaining Nazi water tanks, now festooned with American graffiti. Walk down the first 40 steps, curve to the right around the back of the water tank, and find the next set of steps. Begin walking down, slowly and carefully. Like almost all the staircases on this walk, it is mostly without handrails, and at times becomes extremely steep. Go slowly and enjoy the drop—and a long drop it is. Over multiple sets, interrupted periodically by landings, and lined occasionally by a handrail that used to be the conduit for electrical service, walk down 321 steps.

You land, after a short dirt path, on a wide paved road. This was one of the driveways to the Stephens estate. Turn right, and head up a slight grade. After 100 feet or so, as the road begins to bend to the right, look for a narrow dirt path on the left, marked by a short yucca plant. 10 feet in, you will find the next staircase. Drop down the 130 steps, heavily shaded and, in winter, sometimes bordered by moss, then down a final 47 steps to land within the Nazi camp itself.

Up to the left are the remains of a greenhouse. To the right is the shell of the power station, now a tagger's paradise. Outside and in, the walls are covered with creative signs and slogans, and the basement is ankle-deep with empty paint cans.

Steps just past the power station rise to a concrete platform. Ignore these, and instead walk to the right and up the encampment driveway. A hundred feet up, you'll see what's left of the Stephens-Schmidt guardhouse and fueling station. It's now a mass of crumpled steel walls with a vibrantly rusty collection of cast iron sinks, refrigerator doors, and electric generators stacked on top of one another.

You can explore more of the encampment by following the road to its terminus, then continuing on a footpath that runs along the bottom of the canyon. Upstream is a large barn-like structure behind a chain-link fence, and evidence of driveways, walkways, and other buildings. Considerably farther up you will find Camp Josepho, a Boy Scout facility. Farther still, many miles farther, the fire road you began walking on will meet the unpaved fire road section of Mulholland Drive, which also connects to nearby Mandeville and Temescal Canyon hiking trails.

But for now, turn around and walk back down the driveway, passing the stairs you've just descended, and continue along the paved road. Here, at the bottom of the canyon, are sycamores native to the area and an array of pines probably planted by the Stephens-Schmidt group. Follow the paved road as it rises slightly. Walk past a hard left-hand switchback, and continue straight ahead.

After 100 feet or so, the road begins to turn to the left and rise again. A short, sand-colored wall appears on the right, and a line of six tall, straight pine trees. Twenty feet after the last of these trees and the end of the short wall, you will find a dirt path peeling off to the right. Twenty paces in, you will find the final staircase rising from the underbrush.

This is the monster—the largest known staircase in Los Angeles. Like the other staircases on this walk, it's made of poured concrete, and has no handrails or overhead lighting. In sections, it is quite steep. And it is quite long. It hardly seems fair to say *how* long. Maybe you shouldn't even know how long, until you've climbed it. Begin marching up. Pace yourself. Take advantage of the few flat landings. Enjoy the overhang that shades the lower section of the staircase. Then, when you have finally finished climbing, pat yourself on the back. Did that seem like a lot of steps? It was. It was 512 steps.

One morning at the top of these stairs, I met a man who told me this story: In the mid-1990s, he and three friends pooled $5,000 of their money and set a competition: The first one to successfully run up all 531 steps, two at a time, without slowing or stopping, even for a second, would claim the prize. Each of the four fitness buffs tried multiple times to complete the task. None could do it. The money went unclaimed, and finally the competition was cancelled.

The water tank is on your left. The fence and gate are ahead of you. Step onto the paved road and turn right. Begin the walk back. Now, there are great views of the canyons, the city, and the beach. Up ahead, on the flat piece of mountaintop sitting above everything else, you can see the vast estate owned by Dennis Tito, the scientist-billionaire who is famously known as mankind's first space tourist. In 2001, he orbited the earth 128 times, over seven days, as a passenger on Russia's Soyuz TM-32 spacecraft.

The road begins to drop and the views continue on the right. Walk back past the fire road gate, back onto the paved road below, and up Casale to the corner of Capri, and the end of this excursion. Congratulations!

The walks in this book cover almost all the public staircases in Los Angeles. But some staircases were too remote, or too isolated, to include. In Pasadena, there's a gorgeous set of stairs just above Lacey Park, and in Pacific Palisades there's one off Arno Way, and another linking Via De La Paz to Haverford Avenue, which have no brother staircases to link into a cohesive walk. Laurel Canyon has a couple of fine sets of stairs, too, that go no place and connect to nothing.

There's a beautiful old Chavez Ravine staircase, unearthed by city workers in late 2008, near the intersection of Solano Avenue and Jarvis Street, that may have relatives still buried nearby. Off Heritage Square, near Mt. Washington, there are several good staircases that might make a good walk. An interesting loop could be made of the stairs that rise around York Boulevard and Delevan Drive, and fall again from Banbury Place, in Glassell Park. Around Mt. Angelus, near Figueroa Street and York, there are nine interlinking public staircases dating from the 1920s—but five of them are gated and locked. There's a honey of a staircase in Silver Lake off the western end of Fargo Street, but it's locked, too. So are a dozen more, here and there around the city.

There are a few staircases in San Pedro, and at least one in Mar Vista. On University Hill, near Cal State Los Angeles, the Heidelman stairs rise majestically, but don't quite connect to the El Sereno stairs, which are more than a mile away. Rosewood Terrace is a lovely walk, but has only the Myosotis stairs nearby. There's Altura Walk! And Andes Walk! And Chaucer Walk! Maybe one day I'll be able to weave some of those into a loop, too.

Then, finally, there are the many staircases I've never even seen. *You* know where they are. I'm hoping you'll tell me, so I can make them into more walks for further editions of this book. Please visit http://www.secretstairs-la.com and contribute your questions, comments, and walks.

ACKNOWLEDGEMENTS

There are 235 individual staircases included in the walks in this book, and about 21,000 individual stairs. The 42 circular walks cover more than 110 miles. I have walked all those stairs, all those staircases, and all those miles—multiple times—in the construction of these walks. But I have not walked alone. Julie Singer was my wife, helpmeet, and constant companion, and without her support I would never have begun or completed this project.

Many, many others helped me, too. My fellow stair enthusiast Steve Finkel gave me friendship, guidance, and maps. I learned a lot about local architects from realtors Andy Jelmert and Michael Locke and their online site, the Silver Lake News. My old friend Eric Stone gave me shelter in 1981, in a house on a walk-street that introduced me to the Silver Lake stairs. My stairwalking pals Simone Lueck, Eva Eilenberg, Diana Wagman, Charlotte Hildebrand, and Molly Ruffan walked my walks and corrected my errors. Russell Fleming, Mark Fleming, and Anne Taylor Fleming walked with me. David Fleming tried to educate me about plant life. Sue Horton tried to educate me about bird life. Three dozen others joined me on monthly stairwalks over the last two years. Their enthusiasm, and the success of local travel guides like Erin Mahoney Harris's *Walking L.A.*, convinced me there was a reason for this book to exist.

Still others helped bring it to life. Diane Edwardson led me to staircase documents and historic photographs. Silver Lake historian Bob Herzog provided me with maps. Silver Lake Neighborhood Council officers Jason Lyon, Scott Crawford, and Elizabeth Bougart-Sharkov, and Councilman Tom LaBonge, gave me encouragement. I also benefited tremendously from the work of Larry Gordon and Adah Bakalinsky, whose 1990 guide *Stairway Walks of Los Angeles*, though long out of print, was a great model, and from the work of Dan Koeppel, whose marathon stair-climbing was a great inspiration.

Finally, I owe a debt of gratitude to the staff of Santa Monica Press, and publisher Jeffrey Goldman. He stepped up, signed on, and made the stairs a book.